GET S
for LIFE

GET SLIM *for* LIFE

EDITED BY SASKIA SARGINSON

CAMBRIDGE PUBLISHING GROUP

First published in Great Britain in 1993 by
Cambridge Publishing Group, 20 Perowne Street,
Cambridge CB1 2AY.

Writer/ researcher: Roland Harris
Editor: Saskia Sarginson
Scientific Editor: Dr. Susan Jebb
Typesetting and production: CBA, Cambridge.
Printed in Great Britain by TAS Offset Printing Services, Norwich.
Illustrations by Nik Coole of Purple Pod Productions.
Photography by Rupert Watts

© Cambridge Publishing Group 1993.

British Library Cataloguing-in-Publication Data.
A catalogue record for this book is available from the British Library.

ISBN 0 9520482 0 5

All rights reserved. No part of this publication may be reproduced, stored in a retrieval system, or transmitted in any form or by any means, electronic, mechanical, photocopying, recording or otherwise without the prior permission of Cambridge Publishing Group.

Contents

	Foreword	
	Introduction	1
1	Are you overweight – and why?	3
2	Most diets don't work!	8
3	This diet can be a pleasure	12
4	The fight against fat	17
5	Sugar – the second enemy	22
6	Fibre – your friend for life	26
7	Successful shopping	29
8	Meal planning and eating out	36
9	Clever cooking	42
	Recipe section	47
10	Booze and blubber	69
11	Exercise – is it worth the effort?	71
12	Feeling great – looking good	76
	Food Contents Tables	79
	Further reading	87

Foreword

Get Slim for Life is a book about a lifestyle – a way of life in which the achievement of good health and vitality begins with food. It explains, in simple terms, the reasons why obesity can develop, and why so many diets promising rapid weight loss fail to deliver long term success.

This book is not about a diet in the traditional way of thinking, in which each and every food has to be counted and recorded and where one is 'on' or 'off' a diet. *Get Slim for Life* teaches a style of eating in which, by learning to select foods of low energy density, it is possible to restrict the amount of energy consumed and to reduce the risk of accumulating surplus calories. It demonstrates that such changes need not be difficult or unpleasant; just as many people have already changed from whole milk to lower fat varieties, this book suggests many other ways in which day-to- day eating habits may be modified in the pursuit of slimness and good health.

The recent COMA Report on Dietary Reference Values advised a decrease in fat consumption and an increase in the consumption of complex carbohydrates as a prescription for healthier living. This book shows practical ways to make these changes, along with advice on decreasing the intake of sugars, whilst maintaining the nutritional value of the diet. As such *Get Slim for Life* promotes a style of eating for the whole family – and not just for those trying to lose weight.

Susan A. Jebb BSc, SRD, Ph D.
Medical Research Council, Dunn Nutrition Unit
Cambridge UK.
1992

Introduction

You may wonder if there really is a need for another diet book when bookshelves all over the country are groaning under the weight of numerous volumes that all claim to be the ultimate authority on successful slimming.

The short answer is "Yes there is!" Because only very recently has broad agreement been reached in medical circles over the causes and treatment of obesity and much of this knowledge is still only available in scientific reports and text books. Add to this the growing recognition that most slimming diets – especially the fads and Very Low Calorie Diets – simply don't work in the long term and it seems after all that there *is* room for another diet book. One that explains the latest medical research and weight reduction methods in plain English and recognises that there are no magic short-cuts to losing fat.

This book sets out to guide you gently into a new way of eating, a way of eating that will not unbalance or disturb your body, but that will help you shed unwanted fat to reveal a slimmer figure that you will be able to keep for good.

After understanding just why you are overweight in the first place, you will then discover how you can reach your ideal weight without starving yourself, endangering your health, feeling deprived, ruining your social life or suffering any of the unpleasant side-effects (like bad breath and constipation) that so many other diets involve.

In fact, this book isn't so much about 'dieting' - it's more about finding a new way of eating that goes hand-in-hand with a fresh approach to your lifestyle. After following the advice in this book you will find that you have boundless new energy levels, glowing skin, glossy hair and that elusive slimmer figure that you can now keep FOR LIFE.

CHAPTER 1

Are you overweight – and why?

*I*f you think you are overweight you are certainly not alone. A report, published in 1984, by the Department of Health and Social Security showed that approximately nine million women and almost eleven million men in Great Britain were 'very' overweight. That's over a third of the adult population!

As you might expect, this level of obesity is quite common in the Western World – 34 million Americans for example are classified as 'obese'. Maybe that's why we are known as the 'developed' nations!

Some people will say that they are not the slightest bit unhappy about being fat – they enjoy their food, seem quite content and feel fit enough to cope with life's demands.

For most of us though, the picture isn't quite so pleasant. The thought of wobbling off to catch a bus, squeezing into a swimming costume or attracting the opposite sex just adds insult to obesity.

Most doctors will also agree that being fat is none-too-desirable, but for very different reasons. If you are more than 40% overweight you run twice the risk of dying from disease of the coronary arteries.

Even for less overweight people, it is still beneficial to shed those excess pounds.

Every pound of fat that you lose is one pound less tissue requiring oxygenated blood to be pumped through, thereby reducing strain on the heart and coronary arteries.

But it's not just the strain that's a problem. Studies have shown that obese people are much more likely to develop diabetes as well as the increased levels of blood cholesterol and high blood pressure that contribute to coronary heart disease.

Beyond a shadow of doubt, if you are overweight there are very good reasons to slim down.

Are you overweight?

OK. You think you're overweight – but by how much?

The chart below shows the recommended weight ranges for men and women based on a report by the Royal College of Physicians.

You should weigh yourself on a reliable set of scales wearing indoor clothing but not shoes.

Compare your weight against the column for your height.

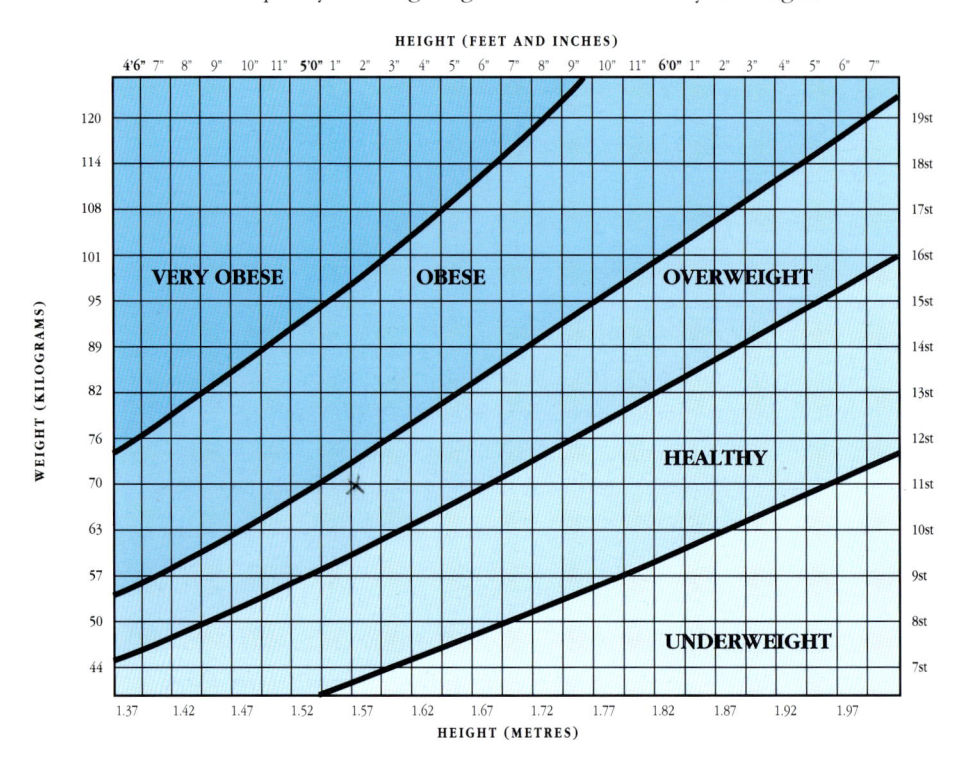

Maybe you're within the healthy weight range for your height but still feel flabby. In that case it's down to muscle tone and condition and it's very straightforward to get trim (see Chapter 11 on Exercise). But if you find yourself overweight then it's time to do something about it.

Right now, you may wonder if it's going to be worth the effort. You may well be someone who's dieted before and failed.

Do read on, because this diet is different. We are not suggesting any fads or famine regimes.

A few simple changes in your lifestyle now could create a whole new sense of well-being – and the figure to go with it.

First though, let's look at the reasons for the extra weight you're carrying.

How do you become overweight?

One thing is clear – there is still a lot to be learnt about obesity because even the experts disagree.

It is possible that you are overweight for genetic or hormonal reasons, in which case you should discuss this with your doctor.

However, such cases are rare.

Some experts believe that fat people have relatively slow metabolisms – that their bodies burn energy at a much lower rate than leaner people of the same weight.

Other experts suggest that overeating is the real problem, while another group claims that lack of exercise is to blame.

So who is right?

Let's examine some facts

Most of the energy we get from food is used as fuel for normal body functions and physical activity. This energy is measured in kilocalories (usually just known as calories). The amount of energy we each require varies from one person to the next. For example, a construction worker might require 3,500 calories a day, whereas a typist would need less than 2,000.

A substantial proportion (about two-thirds) of these calories are used to keep the body functioning and properly maintained. They provide energy for the vital organs – such as heart, lungs, brain, liver and kidneys – for digestion, for maintaining body temperature and for growth.

The amount of energy expended in this way, just to keep the body ticking over, is known as the basal metabolic rate (BMR).

The remaining calories provide energy for physical activity, whether it's manual labour, housework or sports.

The complicating factor is that some people burn energy more quickly than others – they have a higher BMR – and this is closely linked to an individual's size. Bigger people have more to maintain and consequently have higher BMR's.

We become overweight when we eat more food than we need to maintain our BMR and fuel our physical activities.

The excess energy intake is mainly stored as fat, a kind of reserve fuel tank in case of future food shortages.

Luckily for most of us the shortage never arrives and unluckily, the excess fat builds up.

It's at this point though that the theory poses some questions.

We all know of those lucky people who seem to eat huge amounts of food and stay slim. Can their BMR's be so much faster?

Studies with volunteers have demonstrated that indeed, some individuals burn more calories than others of equal weight, even when performing the same physical tasks and taking the same amount of rest.

The hearty eaters, with higher BMR's, were much leaner than than the people with lower BMR's. It really does seem that carrying fat can slow you down – in more ways than one.

Bear in mind too, that many slim and hearty eaters take three meals a day with *nothing* in between. Regular nibbling can load on masses of extra calories.

But are we all stuck with our BMR?

Fortunately, our BMR does not have to be static – the right type of exercise can literally speed-up our system so that we burn more fuel, more quickly.

Can dieting improve our BMR?

Unfortunately, a slimming diet slows down the BMR. The digestion process itself requires 10% of the calories consumed and a Very

Low Calorie Diet can produce a 15% drop in BMR. The body responds to starvation by slowing vital processes, so the less you eat, the less work your body does by itself. That's why it's important to exercise as well, and why a gradual reduction in calories is better than a starvation regime.

Why do we eat too much in the first place?

A big question – with several possible answers!

For many people, the weight problem started in childhood, particularly in the post-war years. Those were the times when hardship ended, when bouncing, rounded, well-fed babies and children were seen as the signs of a healthy new start.

For others, it was the cultivation of a sweet tooth from an early age, when sweets were seen as a special reward and cakes were a teatime treat. The sort of habit that lasts a lifetime.

The trouble is, that when obesity gains an advantage, the problem often becomes hard to stop. The guilt about being overweight can only be eased by the consolation of eating.

Also, the thought of being fat and unattractive often drives some people to indulge even more, because eating becomes the only pleasure left.

Many nutritionists suggest that convenience foods are much to blame. Processed foods often lack nourishment – the 'hidden' sugars and fats have no nutritional value whatsoever – just energy – and these 'empty' calories make up a major part of many people's 'normal' diet.

An important point to remember is that overeating is not necessarily greed or gluttony. Just one digestive biscuit (70 calories) a day in excess of the energy used up through activity adds up to 25,550 calories a year – over 6lbs of fat!

We shall be looking at these problems more closely in later chapters, but the message coming through at this stage is that by choosing the right kind of food and taking a modest amount of exercise, you may not have to eat a great deal less in order to win the battle of the bulge for good!

CHAPTER 2

Most diets don't work!

*L*ast year, around 12.5 million people in the UK put themselves on one kind of diet regime or another.

From high protein to low fat. From high fibre to plain grapefruit. From odd combinations to low calorie 'milkshake' meals. The choices and the conflicting claims are bewildering.

Most of these diets though are either boring, expensive or unsociable, so it's no wonder that 99% of these new dieters either gave up quickly or, eventually failed.

It is tempting to think, after all, that by severely reducing your intake of food you can quickly reach a much lower weight and then stay there by being careful in future.

This simply doesn't happen.

Medical research has shown that after just a short period of time your body will recognise the diet as a sign of starvation and actually start to protect the stores of energy (fat) that you already have.

"But I know of people who lost pounds by crash dieting!"

We have all heard of people who have lost 10 pounds, or even more, in a week through strict dieting. If we don't actually know them we have read their true stories in the diet food manufacturers' advertisements.

But are these stories true? Well, yes they are. But what these people have mostly lost is fluid and muscle tissue, not fat. Unfortunately, the fluid is not just excess water – it contains glycogen, a type of natural sugar that provides much of the 'instant' energy that our bodies require.

Deprived of glycogen, the body slows down, resulting in tiredness, depression and irritability – all common complaints among dieters.

Glycogen also controls the appetite, its loss will trigger sensations of extreme hunger – even though you might have just eaten.

The result is that most crash dieters succeed in losing weight, but then give in to acute hunger pangs soon afterwards and quickly put the pounds back on.

Let's look more closely at some of these so-called 'wonder diets'.

Low Carbohydrate Diets

Once a very popular way of losing weight, low carbohydrate diets were apparently very successful but are now generally recognised as being medically unsound.

A massive reduction in carbohydrate foods (such as bread, pasta, rice and potatoes) does indeed lead to rapid weight loss.

When carbohydrates are cut out from your normal diet, blood glucose (glycogen) has to be maintained from other reserves.

In the early days of such a diet, the glycogen is taken from reserves of fat, but the same process that breaks down fat also breaks down the glycogen stored in the muscles of the body and in the liver. Each molecule of glycogen is linked to four times its weight in water so the weight loss is no longer just fat – it's muscle tissue and water. Low carbohydrate levels also lead to depletion of the body's sodium level. The body then sheds water to balance out the sodium loss. So again, it's water that's being lost, not fat.

The side effects of a low carbohydrate diet can be very unpleasant, in fact they are similar to the symptoms seen in diabetes – hypoglycaemia (low blood sugar) and ketosis (excess blood ketone levels). This often results in light headedness, fatigue, nausea and bad breath. Added to this is the inevitable constipation due to lack of dietary fibre (see Chapter 6). And if you enjoy a drink or two, alcohol can make the effects much worse.

Then how about low protein diets?

The type of diet that cuts out protein – not just meat, fish, and dairy produce, but beans, nuts, pulses and potatoes as well – has often been recommended over the years in one form or another.

It is seen for example, in the fruit-only diet, the salad-only diet and in the more extreme high-fibre diets. This kind of diet can certainly help you lose weight, but again, it's not just fat that disappears.

When protein is restricted, all your body's protein-rich tissue is affected and this includes muscles, heart, liver and spleen.

This tissue is broken down to provide the essential amino acids for more vital body processes such as digestion and antibodies for the immune system.

Eventually, without protein, even these vital processes slow down so that digestion becomes sluggish and the immune system is weakened, reducing your resistance to infections and disease.

It's not the sort of diet that doctors recommend these days!

Fat-burning enzymes?

Somehow, the grapefruit has gained a reputation as a successful slimming aid.

It's been said that grapefruit contains 'enzymes' which somehow break-down body fat but it's much more likely that their success is due to the low protein effect that we have just looked at.

Even if an enzyme was present, it would never directly reach the fat reserves.

That's because enzymes are protein. They are digested in the stomach and small intestine, absorbed as amino acids and delivered straight to the liver.

But that's enough of the dieting fads – let's now take a look at the most popular form of weight reduction – the calorie controlled diet.

Does calorie counting work?

Calories are a way of measuring the energy content of food, so the more calories we eat the more energy we have available.

We have already seen that when taking in more energy than we require each day (overeating) the surplus may be stored (as fat) for later use.

This is why so many dieting methods recommend calorie control, to try and plan a way of taking in less energy than we are actually using and so start to drain the energy reserve that is stored as fat.

In theory this should work, but unfortunately it's not quite as simple as that – calorie counting is time-consuming and virtually impossible to maintain accurately with today's busy lifestyles.

After all, who can establish precisely the amount of energy that is required day-by-day for activity *and* make sure they take in less than they need.

And when you think of the side effects of dieting – stress, depression, food obsession, headaches, constipation, bad breath and low energy – it's hardly the way to improve your appearance or enhance your sex appeal!

So, what's the answer?

Medical opinion is united in recommending a gradual approach to weight loss. This gives the body time to adjust gently by avoiding the starvation signs. Through a sensible, balanced diet of wholesome foods, low in fat and sugar, many people are able to lose weight steadily and effectively.

Most of us will also need the extra boost that comes from increased activity and exercise.

There is no magical formula for losing weight but by following the advice in the rest of this book you will soon learn the principles of sensible eating and moderate exercise that will make you slimmer and fitter FOR LIFE.

CHAPTER 3

This diet can be a pleasure

We have just seen how most slimming diets are usually destined to fail.

They either impose impossible demands on your body or impossible demands on your lifestyle. Nobody wants to go through starvation, deprivation, bad moods or fatigue just to get slim and we are not recommending that you should.

As we have seen, if you do put yourself through deprivation or strange combinations to shed weight there's a 99% chance that your body will later react with food cravings that will pile the pounds back on.

There's no point in carefully counting the calories in every meal you make or eating a simple salad by yourself while the rest of the family tuck-in to something substantial.

Food is here to be enjoyed. Eating should be a pleasure, not a source of guilt!

"How can I enjoy food and still lose weight?"

It's simple – by choosing the right kind of food and making time for a reasonable level of activity or exercise you will lose weight.

This weight loss won't be water or lean muscle tissue either – it will be fat that disappears.

This may sound too good to be true, but read on ...

What is the wrong kind of food?

Our 'normal' diet in Western countries is heavily based on fats and sugars – much of them hidden in convenience and processed foods.

Our Western diet is also low in fibre – much to the detriment of our general health and well-being.

These facts are not new or revolutionary. They have been the subject of many expert books and medical papers in recent years.

Two of these publications have received quite extensive media coverage: the COMA reports (Committee on Medical Aspects of Food Policy) on Diet and Cardiovascular Disease, and on Dietary Reference Values.

Although the Committee was looking at different areas of health – one on diet-related diseases and the other on nutrition – their recommendations are remarkably similar.

They both suggest that we, as a nation, should be eating much less fat, less sugar, less salt and more fibre. You may wonder what this has to do with losing weight but we shall be taking a closer look at the reasons for this in the next three chapters – that is apart from salt, which has little to do with weight loss, but a lot to do with hypertension (high blood pressure) and is therefore best reduced for reasons of general health.

What is the right kind of food?

Curiously enough, one of the right kinds of food is exactly what the diet books used to try and persuade us to stop eating – the complex carbohydrates!

Bread, rice, cereals, pasta and potatoes were all once regarded as fattening, but just how wrong can you get?

These complex carbohydrates are extremely low in fat and sugar – it's the creamy sauces and knobs of butter we add that load on the fat.

The wholemeal versions of these foods are also high in fibre – especially bread and cereals.

What's more, they are filling – they will satisfy your hunger without providing surplus calories. They also provide plenty of lasting energy – the body slowly converts them to glycogen, the essential blood-sugar fuel.

However, as we saw in the last chapter, carbohydrates alone do not provide adequate nourishment – nor a great deal of gastronomic delight!

As we stress throughout this book, it's moderation and balance that are important.

By combining a modest amount of low fat meat or fish – and as much fresh fruit and vegetables as you wish – with any of the complex carbohydrates, you will find that excess weight just disappears – not overnight, but gradually and permanently.

The important thing is to remember that as far as possible, you should be eating wholefoods. This means avoiding quite a few of the pre-packed convenience goods in favour of fresh, unprocessed, undisguised ingredients.

In today's shopping environment this is not always as easy as it sounds – the following chapters will show you where some of the problems lie.

However, it's not impossible to find good butchers who sell game and trim meat properly, or good bakers of wholesome bread or greengrocers with really fresh produce.

In fact, many supermarkets have now sharpened-up their approach to wholefoods and freshness with improved quality control procedures and full labelling of contents.

"Won't this cost me a fortune?"

Some items, such as lean, trimmed meat, will cost a little more per pound, but then you're not paying for the useless fat!

Other meat, such as game birds, are more expensive than chicken – but these are really a treat.

Most of the healthier options that we suggest are actually cheaper in the long run.

Poultry and fish for example, are incredibly good value when compared to red meats.

The complex carbohydrates such as pasta, bread and potatoes are cheap and filling.

Fresh fruit and vegetables usually cost less than canned or frozen versions.

All in all you should actually save!

"Sounds like I'll be stuck in the kitchen!"

If you are used to take-away or ready-made meals then maybe you'll need extra time in the kitchen..

Otherwise, you won't really notice the difference. You'll save time by not having to peel potatoes but you'll spend a little longer skimming fat from gravies or casseroles.

What we are really concerned with is avoiding fat and sugar, not creating domestic chores.

There are now many frozen and canned varieties that avoid added sugar or fat, so it's a question of reading the labels (but more of this in Chapter 7 and at the end of the book).

"Well, there must be some drawbacks?"

There are no drawbacks to eating wholesome foods, low in fat and sugar.

Not only will you lose weight but your health will improve as well.

The main difficulty is going to be avoiding things like cream cakes, chocolate buns, cheeseburgers and the crackling on roast pork!

Let's face it – there are no short-cuts to losing weight. There is no magical 'medicine' that will let you carry on eating exactly what you want and 'neutralise' the calories so that you don't gain weight.

The fact is, that if you are overweight, you will have to make some changes in your ways of eating and exercise if you want to be slim.

BUT, you don't have to suffer to get there.

"But how can a diet be a pleasure?"

What we are really talking about is a whole new approach to life. Now is the time to take a close look at your eating and exercise habits and see what a few simple changes can do to transform your appearance and your well-being.

The right balance between diet and exercise will guarantee that you will not only shed those excess pounds but maintain your slim new figure for life.

You will also benefit from better circulation, improved posture, healthier skin and hair, bright-eyes and boundless new energy.

As you achieve lower body weight and better digestion, your whole system will improve – especially if you take regular exercise as outlined in Chapter 11.

This means that you can enjoy the occasional treat – the birthday or Christmas meal with all the trimmings; the odd box of chocolates you might receive; the once-in-a-while cream cake.

Remember too that the amount of food you eat will vary quite naturally from day to day, so don't feel guilty about the occasional lapse from the ideal diet. Just balance out any over indulgence with well-controlled days when your self-discipline is strong.

This diet is not about depriving yourself of enjoyment – in fact, once you discover the taste of real food you will lose your appetite for junk. Fat will taste fatty and sugar will taste, well, sugary.

This is the answer to all of those old dieting problems – enjoy your food in moderate quantity and never at the expense of quality.

CHAPTER 4

The fight against fat

There is an old saying, 'you are what you eat' and there is more than a grain of truth in this.

We have already seen how a great proportion of the population in the Western World is very overweight and it's no coincidence that the Western diet is extremely high in fats and sugars when compared to less affluent societies.

We have also seen that dietary fat is not just responsible for excess body weight – it is a major contributor to heart disease, the single biggest cause of death in Great Britain.

The problem lies in high blood cholesterol levels which are often caused by eating too many saturated fats.

In fact, there is general agreement among the various medical and food advisory committees that we should all reduce our intake of saturated fats by half.

However, this only applies to *saturated* fats. There are other groups of fats – the polyunsaturates – that are positively essential for good health.

Which fat should we be fighting?

There are many types of fats, but roughly speaking, they can be divided into three groups: saturated, monounsaturated and polyunsaturated.

It is however, impossible to isolate each one separately in the food we eat since no source of dietary fat is made up from one single group.

For example, butter is generally regarded as a saturated fat but it actually contains 54% saturated, 20% monounsaturated and 3% polyunsaturated fats.

By comparison, a typical soft margarine 'high in polyunsaturates' contains 14% saturated, 26% monounsaturated and 40% polyunsaturated fats.

It is therefore impossible to cut out saturated fats completely, but as the example shows it is possible to make very significant adjustments in favour of polyunsaturates.

For the purposes of this diet we can regard saturated fats as the main enemy. Monounsaturated fats are neutral and polyunsaturated fats are our allies – they are essential for body functions and they can actually help to reduce blood cholesterol levels.

How can we tell the difference?

Generally speaking, saturated fats remain solid at room temperature while polyunsaturates stay liquid.

Thus, the heavily saturated fats include butter, lard, solid margarine, cheese and the fat that surrounds lean meat.

Polyunsaturates include olive oil, sunflower oil, soya oil and corn oil.

In practice, it is often difficult to establish the levels of saturated or polyunsaturated fats just by appearance.

For example cream and coconut oil are high in saturated fats while 'fatty' fish such as salmon, trout, herring and sardines are high in polyunsaturates.

Similarly, we can trim the 'fat' off meat, but even the leanest beef is still 6% fat and the average grilled lamb chop is more like 30%.

Then of course there are the 'hidden' fats in all types of food. Not just the obvious things like sausages and pork pies, but the 20% that you'll find in plain biscuits!

Where do we find saturated fats?

Virtually all the highly saturated fats are derived from meat and dairy products. Although saturated fats are present in fish and vegetable oils the levels are very much lower.

The problem in defining fatty foods is complicated by the 'hidden' fats – the fats that are used in cakes and biscuits, the oils that are used to fry potato snacks and the 'dairy' part that makes up chocolate bars.

Use the Food Contents Tables at the end of the book to find out the levels of fat in the food you eat.

How do we avoid fat in food?

The first priority must be to cut down on meat and especially meat-based products such as pies and sausages.

Instead, go for poultry, game – including pheasant, partridge, pigeon, rabbit, hare and venison – fish and shellfish. These are all low in saturated fats, they are not expensive in comparison with lamb or beef and they are definitely quite a treat.

Also, substitute vegetable or pulse-based dishes for at least two main meals each week. Don't be put off by the thought of 'going vegetarian', the recipes we give in Chapter 9 will appeal to even the most traditional meat-eating male.

Next, cut down on high-fat dairy foods. Change right away to skimmed or semi-skimmed milk and see if you can adjust occasionally to lemon tea, jasmine tea, herbal teas or black coffee.

Instead of cream, use yoghurt or fromage frais.

Switch to low fat margarine instead of butter- make sure it's high in polyunsaturates.

Look for low fat cheese and cottage cheese – or better still, follow a meal with fresh fruit instead!

Cut down on cakes, biscuits and confectionery which contain around 40% of their energy as fat.

How do we avoid fat in cooking?

Many methods of cooking actually succeed in *adding* fat to otherwise healthy food.

An extreme example is cod or plaice, deep fried in batter, the basis of good old English fish and chips.

The fish itself is excellent, containing just a little over 1% fat if grilled or baked. The batter mix of eggs, milk and flour can boost the fat content of deep-fried fish to something nearer 40%, since a great deal of the cooking fat is absorbed as well.

Point number one therefore, is throw away your deep-fat fryer!

Next, keep a careful watch on the frying pan! This is another way of adding fat to food.

For example, a fried rasher of bacon contains around 42% fat but by grilling it, the fat content can be *reduced* to 35%. Similarly, a fried egg to go with the bacon will be around 20% fat, but if it was poached instead, the fat content would be nearer 10%.

The message is: avoid adding fat to any food and switch to cooking methods that will *reduce* the fat levels in meat.

The trouble is that we've all grown to enjoy fried foods, they are undeniably delicious! Without a doubt, this is a difficult step to take but it *is* important. By changing your style of cooking you can make a significant difference to the amount of fat you eat.

After a short time you will actually appreciate the *improvement* in your cooking. Frying and deep-frying actually disguise the true flavours of fresh ingredients and fried food will soon start to taste too greasy.

However, there may be times when you simply can't resist something fried. Well, go ahead and enjoy it – this diet is not about deprivation and boredom.

What you can do to keep a clear conscience is avoid using butter, margarine or lard. Ideally, choose olive or vegetable oil – use it sparingly – and drain food well before puting it on the plate.

Also, try to use a heavy-based non-stick pan – you can then use far less oil than usual.

Another style of frying that you can enjoy is the Chinese method of stir-frying – this is explained in Chapter 9, along with other useful guidelines for avoiding fat.

To summarise, avoid fried food as much as possible – especially deep fried.

With meat, go for grilling, roasting or stewing. When grilling and roasting, place the meat on a rack and allow the fat to drain away. When stewing, skim off the surface fat before serving. This goes for gravy and sauces too.

With 'dry' meats, such as poultry and game, use olive or vegetable oil for marinading and basting – then drain the meat well after cooking.

For fish, try grilling or oven baking in foil (this is really delicious because all the flavours, juices and goodness are retained).

Is there any danger of eating too little fat?

The fact is that saturated fats are of no nutritional benefit whatsoever – they are positively bad for you due to the effect they have on blood cholesterol levels.

The essential fats – the polyunsaturates – are vital for maintaining body function but the average adult daily requirement (10 grams) is very low.

Polyunsaturates are not just found in fish, game and poultry – they are present in bread, nuts, cereals and some vegetables. It is virtually impossible, even on the most spartan diet, to avoid less than 10 grams of essential fats each day.

HEARTFELT BENEFIT

Too much fat in food means too much fat in your body – not just as excess flab, but in the blood–fat cholesterol.

High cholesterol levels lead to the arterial disease that causes strokes and heart attacks.

Fat is your number one enemy – eating less will improve your health.

CHAPTER 5

Sugar – the second enemy

*E*ach year, around 100lbs of sugar is consumed for every individual person in Great Britain.

We have been led to believe that sugar is essential for good health and that it gives us bags of energy. But how true is this?

Sugar is indeed a useful source of energy for highly active people such as athaletes, but for those of us trying to lose weight it is of no value at all!

Why is sugar unhealthy?

Let's first decide what is *sugar*.

For a start, all carbohydrates are composed of sugar – and this includes starch in bread, potatoes, rice and pasta which is slowly absorbed in digestion and converted to glucose in the blood.

Other types of natural sugar include lactose from milk, and glucose and fructose which are present in most types of fruit, some vegetables and in honey.

What we mean by sugar as the second enemy is the refined, processed stuff that's available in packets on the supermarket shelves and hidden away in cakes, confectionery, soft drinks and a host of convenience foods.

It doesn't matter whether it's brown or white, crystals or syrup, it's totally devoid of nutrients. No vitamins, no minerals, no protein or fibre, it has no nutritional value at all!

Refined sugar is in fact nothing but energy and, the danger is that it's so easy to consume.

In Chapter 1 we looked at the reasons for obesity and sugar was a major cause. It's always been a treat in sweets and cakes and once a 'sweet tooth' develops it's amazingly difficult to change.

Sugar is just empty calories. It's easy to take in a massive surplus of energy which, unless you're doing an enormous amount of exercise, goes back into the body's reserve as (you've guessed it!) FAT.

How much sugar is healthy?

All the sugar we need each day can easily be supplied from natural sources such as bread, potatoes, pasta, fruit, milk and vegetables.

The sugar we add to drinks, or consume in sweets and cakes is likely to be entirely surplus to our needs.

In fact, it's far more beneficial to get our sugar through natural forms, especially the slow-release sugar in starches, and avoid the sudden surges in blood sugar levels that arrive after consuming refined sugar in food and drinks.

As with fats, some expert committees have advised that we should all reduce our intake of sugar by half.

This is not just a remedy for obesity. Sugar is a primary cause of tooth decay and it's over-consumption is also linked to other disorders including raised cholesterol levels.

In fact, some nutritional experts and virtually all dentists would prefer us to eliminate refined sugars from our diet altogether.

How do we avoid refined sugar?

The first step is obvious – think before reaching for the sugar bowl. Gradually reduce the amount of sugar in hot drinks until you no longer need it at all. Once you get used to it, you will probably prefer the taste.

Next, avoid sweets and confectionery. Try not to keep sweets, chocolates or biscuits in the house, and certainly avoid giving them to children as rewards or treats.

If you *must* have a nibble between meals try fresh fruit, dried fruit, raw vegetables or grissini (bread sticks).

Also, cut out all canned drinks and fruit squashes – they are extremely high in sugar. Go for fruit juice diluted with sparkling mineral water instead.

Avoid adding sugar to food – resist the temptation to glaze carrots or peas with sugar or butter. If you are stewing fresh fruit make sure you taste it first – a teaspoon of honey is probably quite enough instead of two tablespoons of sugar.

Watch out for sauces as well. Tomato ketchup contains up to 33% sugar and mint or cranberry jelly is almost 70%.

The list of hidden sugars is endless. Manufacturers today seem to add sugar to everything – even pickle and ready-made salads may have added sugar.

It is really much better to avoid processed and convenience foods unless they clearly contain no added sugars.

The Food Contents Tables at the end of the book will also help you to spot the hidden sugars – otherwise read the labels carefully because sugar is often disguised under different names, mostly ending in 'ose': sucrose, glucose, dextrose, fructose, maltose as well as caramel and sorbitol.

Every meal of the day is under attack from the second enemy, so let's take a look at a typical day and see how to avoid the hidden threat.

Breakfast:

Fruit juice. Cereal. Toast and marmalade. Coffee.

Well, there's obviously sugar in the marmalade (around 69%) and you don't have to add it to the coffee – but there's even more lurking in this simple meal.

For example, a litre carton of fruit juice can have up to 15 grams of sugar added before it has to be labelled as 'sweetened'.

Cereals are the biggest surprise though – and not just the Sugar Puffs, Sugar Smacks and Coco Pops. All Bran has 15% sugar and a typical muesli 26%! Even worse, some of the new 'healthy' low fat cereals with fruit, nuts and fibre contain up to 43% sugar!

The answer is to read those labels carefully – make sure the fruit juice is unsweetened, check the cereal for added sugar and switch to a low-sugar jam.

Lunch:

Chicken salad sandwich. Fruit yoghurt. Slice of fruit cake. Can of fizzy drink.

The chicken salad sandwich is fine. Fruit yoghurt though, may be something of a surprise. Most fruit yoghurt in this country contains up to 15% sugar and that's often more than the fruit content! Go for natural yoghurt with a piece of fresh fruit instead.

Well, you expect to find some sugar in a slice of plain fruit cake, but would you expect 43%? That's the average. Far better to have a plain scone or teacake instead.

As for the drink, it's disastrous! A typical can of fizzy drink contains the equivalent of seven teaspoons of sugar and so-called 'athletic' energy drinks have even more.

Fruit juice with mineral water is a far better choice.

Evening Meal:

Grilled lamb chop, green beans, carrots and new potatoes. Tinned peaches with ice cream.

As long as you avoid glazing the carrots and having mint jelly with the lamb, the main course is fine as far as sugar goes. The dessert though, is something else! Canned fruit syrup can contain as much added sugar as cola drinks. Look for the natural juice variety or, better still, buy fresh fruit instead.

Ice cream of course, is another source of sugar – even vanilla is 12% sugar and choc chip or caramel varieties can reach 30%.

If you have grown up with sugar and enjoy the taste you are almost certainly addicted. In this respect, sugar is as bad as alcohol or cigarettes although less immediately damaging to your health.

If you seriously want to lose weight you must accept that sugar is as bad as fat – and where the two meet, as in cakes, biscuits and desserts, the threat to your figure is doubled!

Aim to reduce your sugar intake right away, but do it gradually. Give your body and your taste buds time to adapt – that way you can avoid desperate cravings.

At first, simply move to less sugary items. Go for plain biscuits or doughnuts instead of the jam and cream varieties.

Finish a meal with naturally sweet fruit such as pineapple, banana or grapes instead of sweet, creamy desserts.

Gently reduce the amount of sugar you add to hot drinks.

Make your own naturally sweet jam (the recipes are in Chapter 9).

Given time, you will be amazed how your taste can change. You will find fizzy drinks disgusting and heavy desserts just too much.

At this stage you will be winning - and feeling much better as well.

CHAPTER 6

Fibre – your friend for life

A great deal has been written in recent years about the importance of fibre – indeed entire diets, such as the F-Plan, have been based around its benefits.

The surprising thing is, that fibre has no nutritional value. Just like fat and sugar, fibre contributes no vitamins, no protein and no minerals. Unlike fat and sugar though, fibre has no calories – it provides no energy at all.

What's the point in eating fibre?

The body cannot absorb or digest fibre and this is its primary benefit.

Fibre adds bulk to our diet – it absorbs between 5 and 15 times its own weight of water.

Fibre travels quickly through the system, absorbing harmful waste products on its way and helps keep the digestive tract healthy.

A shortage of dietary fibre leads directly to constipation, a uniquely Western problem. Nearly 20% of British people take laxatives whereas peasant populations don't need them at all.

But it's not just constipation that's the problem. The build-up of toxic wastes in the system may lead to disorders of the gut and cancers of the colon and bowel – the so-called 'diseases of civilisation'. These diseases are virtually unknown in more 'primitive' societies.

For those of us trying to lose weight, fibre has another important benefit – it makes us chew food longer and bulks out the stomach. This makes us feel satisfied more quickly (and stops us overeating) without supplying surplus energy.

Our average diet in Western countries is notoriously low in fibre. Meats, cheese, eggs, sausages, chips, burgers, sweets, and cakes are all virtually free of fibre.

It's very important, not just as a slimming aid but for general health, to boost your fibre intake each day – for life!

Which foods provide fibre?

Fibre is found entirely in plants – grains, leaf and root vegetables, fruits, beans, peas and other pulses – particularly in the stems, seed coats and leaves.

Unprocessed grains are thought to be the best source of dietary fibre and these are found in foods such as wholemeal bread, muesli, porridge oats and brown rice.

Processed flour products such as white bread, cakes, white rice and pasta have around 85% of the fibre removed during processing – you would therefore have to eat six times as much white bread to get the same amount of fibre as wholemeal.

Nuts are also high in fibre – even peanuts are over 8% fibre and almonds have more than 14%. The drawback is that they are also high in fat – although it's mainly polyunsaturated – and calories.

Fruit and most vegetables, particularly when raw or lightly cooked are another important source of fibre. It's better not to peel them either whenever possible because the peel itself is rich in fibre, especially in the case of potatoes.

"My family won't like wholemeal bread and brown rice!"

If your family is only used to white bread then try introducing some wholemeal as an occasional treat – they might get to like it!

If you must stick to white, go for the better quality bread from a traditional baker with poppy, caraway or sesame seeds on top.

Alternatively, try granary bread, it's lighter than wholemeal, with three times the fibre of white.

Similarly with baking – if you don't want to switch to wholemeal flour try a 50-50 mixture with white, the result will be a lot more interesting.

Brown rice has been the butt of a number of jokes – usually about hippies or vegetarians! Their reasons for eating it though are entirely sound, and if properly cooked, it tastes a good deal better than you might think – especially the Basmati rice from the Himalayas which has a slim grain and a wonderfully nutty flavour. It's great for making stuffings for poultry, marrow or green peppers as well as an excellent accompaniment to curries and casseroles. If you don't tell your family what it is, they'll think it's an exotic treat!

> ### *HEARTFELT BENEFIT*
> There is some evidence that eating oat porridge reduces blood cholesterol. It is also suggested that beans, pulses and wholewheat foods have the same effect.

The same goes for pasta. The brown (wholemeal) varieties are substantially higher in fibre than white and although they might look strange at first, they're well worth trying.

"How much fibre should I eat each day?"

The average British diet, as we have already seen, contains an inadequate amount of fibre. On average, we are said to eat around 11–13 grams each day, although vegetarians will probably consume more that twice this amount.

The Government's expert committees suggest that we increase our fibre intake to at least 18 grams each day.

You can refer to the Food Contents Tables at the end of the book to find out the fibre content of most types of food.

CHAPTER 7

Successful shopping

*I*n the last three chapters, we have seen just how well the fats and sugars are disguised in packaged and processed foods and how easy it is to avoid essential dietary fibre.

The aim of successful shopping is to avoid products that are high in saturated fats or sugar and select the healthier alternatives.

It is also important, as we have seen, to try and buy food that will provide an adequate daily intake of fibre.

The first step though, is to make an honest assessment of the kind of food that you have been eating and see where immediate improvements can be made.

For some people, the kind of changes that are required will not be too difficult. For others it's going to be quite an adjustment.

If you are accustomed to food that's high in fat or sugar, then make the changes gradually. Give your body and your taste buds time to adjust to the fact that fried foods, sweets and desserts may no longer be quite the same.

Start by choosing leaner cuts of meat. Switch to polyunsaturated margarine instead of butter. Use olive oil or vegetable oil for cooking. Try and avoid added sugars, whether it's in yoghurt, fruit juice, breakfast cereal or TV dinners. Buy plain wholemeal biscuits instead of fancy iced or chocolate ones. Start to introduce fish or game instead of butcher's meat and include at least one vegetarian main meal each week.

This way, you will find it much easier to adjust to the taste and texture of healthier meals without experiencing cravings for the wrong kind of food.

Similarly, it's sensible to increase your fibre intake gently, rather than making sure you eat 18 grams a day from tomorrow – that way you should avoid any indigestion problems.

First, start by switching to wholemeal or granary bread. Then introduce natural muesli or sugar-free high-fibre breakfast cereal after a week or two. This, when combined with the fibre you eat in vegetables and fruit, will ensure that you gradually build up to a healthy daily amount.

"How do I avoid the wrong kind of food?"

We've already seen some examples of the worst kinds of foods and in general they are easy to avoid or reduce.

Processed meats and dairy products are high in saturated fats.

Cakes, biscuits and confectionery are extremely high in both sugar and fat.

The difficulty is in spotting the 'hidden' fats and sugar in processed and convenience foods.

The section at the end of this book shows the fat, sugar and fibre content of most kinds of food including many of the ready-made and packaged products.

You can use the tables to identify the healthier options before you go shopping, but if in doubt your should refer to the product labels.

By law, manufacturers have to list the ingredients of their food products in exact order of quantity. The highest content is shown first and the lowest last – this certainly helps in spotting fat or sugar-rich foods.

However, the nutrition information, when shown, is a much more useful guide to help you establish the relative contents, and some examples are shown on the following page:

POTATO CRISPS

Typical Nutrition Information		
	Per 100g	Per 30g pack
Energy	2228kJ	668kJ
	533kcal	160kcal
Protein	6.5g	1.9g
Carbohydrate	40.1g	12.0g
Fat	36.8g	11.0g

TWIGLETS
A Healthier Choice

NUTRITION INFORMATION		
Typical Values	per 100g	per TWIGLET
Energy	1620kJ/384kcal	17kJ/4kcal
Protein	12.0g	0.13g
Carbohydrate	62.1g	0.65g
Fat	11.4g	0.12g

TZATZIKI
A Healthier Choice

NUTRITION INFORMATION	
	TYPICAL VALUES
	PER 100g (3½ oz)
ENERGY	100k. CALORIES
	420k. JOULES
PROTEIN	7.5g
CARBOHYDRATE AVAILABLE	7.1g
TOTAL FAT	4.9g
DIETARY FIBRE	1.9g
ADDED SALT	0.4g

CHEESE DIP

Nutritional data per 100g
Energy 1445kJ/350kcal, Protein 6.9g,
Carbohydrates 6.0g.
Fat 33.3g (of which saturated fat 8.8g)

As you can see, the nutrition information is usually shown in grams per 100 grams of product, ie the percentage of each nutrient.

The energy content is also shown in both kilojoules (KJ) and Kilocalories (Kcal) - the latter is what we usually refer to as just 'calories'.

The nutrients are listed under protein, carbohydrate, fat, sodium (salt) and fibre.

The problem is that carbohydrate includes sugar as well as starch, and fat includes saturated, monounsaturated and polyunsaturated fats.

Most reputable manufacturers will distinguish clearly between the types of fats and sugars, but this is not always the case and you have to be particularly careful with added sugar that is just passed-off under the general heading of carbohydrates.

Fats are usually easier to determine, since the ingredients will show if vegetable oils are used and you will know if the food itself is meat or dairy-based.

Bread, cakes and cereals

Choose wholemeal bread in preference to white. Use wholemeal flour in baking (or 50/50 with white). Avoid white flour cakes, biscuits, buns and particularly croissants or cream cakes which are high in saturated fat. If you must continue with biscuits, look for plain, wholemeal varieties maybe with dried fruit added.

Beware of the 'healthy' breakfast cereals – many of the new nut, fruit and fibre mixes are stacked with unnecessary added sugars.

Try brown rice and pasta instead of white.

Fats, oils and dressings

Avoid butter and solid margarine – choose a soft margarine, high in polyunsaturates instead.

Never buy lard or dripping – choose vegetable oils such as sunflower, corn or soya for cooking.

Avoid mayonnaise, salad cream and manufactured dressings – the first is high in saturated fat and the others tend to be loaded with sugar.

Buy olive or walnut oil and make your own dressing with lemon juice or wine vinegar and herbs instead (see Chapter 9).

HEARTFELT BENEFIT

Olive oil is thought to be of positive benefit in keeping down levels of blood cholesterol because it combines 70% unsaturated and 11% polyunsaturated fats which help to break down body fat through chemical interaction.

Meat and poultry

Buy less red meat – choose smaller quantities of well-trimmed (lean) beef, lamb or pork.

Switch to poultry or game (and fish) in preference to red meat. This can include chicken, turkey, guinea fowl, duck, pheasant, partridge, pigeon, grouse, venison, wild boar, hare and rabbit.

In general, buy the whole, natural product and avoid processed or tinned meats such as corned beef, luncheon meat, salami, sausages and burgers.

Processed and tinned meats are very high in saturated fat and salt. The same applies to pâtés, pies and pasties.

Fish

Again, go for the whole, natural product. Buy fish that's as fresh as you can possibly get – look for clean bright eyes, red shining gills and firm flesh. Avoid anything with dull eyes, dry skin or slimy looking flesh.

It really doesn't matter what fish you choose – they are all highly nutritious and the fat in fish is actually good for your health.

Unlike meat products, tinned fish is actually OK – it is usually preserved in vegetable oils or brine and contains little saturated fat.

Shellfish is also an excellent choice, like all fish, it is rich in nutrients and provides a delicious alternative to meat.

The only 'fishy' area in this section is processed fish products. This includes fish fingers, fishcakes and all breaded or battered fish products. Although fish fingers are a good deal healthier than sausages, the breadcrumbs or batter will contain saturated fats to bind them and they will of course absorb even more fat if they are fried.

Fish pâtés though, are high in saturated fat since they are usually extended with cream cheese. Taramosalata is the possible exception since it is usually extended with olive oil and is low in saturated fat.

Eggs and dairy products

Try to buy fewer eggs – the yolk is one of the most concentrated sources of dietary cholesterol – aim to eat less than 3 each week.

Buy fresh skimmed or semi-skimmed milk and avoid evaporated or condensed milk which is high in fat and sugar.

Avoid cream completely. Buy natural yoghurt as a 'creamy' topping for desserts and fromage frais for use in stews or sauces.

Choose low or medium-fat cheeses. Cottage cheese for example contains only 4% fat in comparison to the 33% in cheddar. Many supermarkets now offer ranges of half-fat cheese and a typical cheddar version would be around 16% fat.

Buy natural yoghurt for desserts – it's delicious when combined with fresh fruit and nuts or whipped-up into a 'mousse' with stewed fruit and egg whites (see Chapter 9).

Avoid buying manufactured desserts, whips, mousses and fruit fools, they are all high in fats and sugar.

Fruit and vegetables

Buy more fruit and vegetables, especially fresh ones. Think about their use in salads as well as for main meals.

When buying tinned or frozen versions, watch out for added sugars. Choose the natural juice varieties of tinned fruit and sugar-free frozen food instead.

Buy a small supply of dried fruit to replace sweets and confectionery.

Stock up with dried beans and pulses when you've read the recipes in chapter 9. Not only are they low in fat and sugar and high in fibre, but they are a useful, low-cost way to 'beef-up' a stew and use less meat.

Jams, pickles and sauces

In general, buy low-sugar fruit preserves (or make your own from the recipes in Chapter 9) instead of jam. They will need to be stored in the refrigerator since they have less added sugar to make them keep.

With pickles and sauces, read the labels carefully and avoid the hidden sugars.

Snacks, crisps and nuts

Avoid most potato and corn-based snack products, they are high in fats and salt. If you can't avoid them altogether, look for low-fat crisps, tortilla chips, pretzels and grissini (bread sticks) - buy the lowest fat versions you can find.

Alternatively, buy a few natural nuts, ideally in their shells – but avoid the roasted, salted or dry-roasted versions with added oil and salt. Go easy on the nuts though, they're high in fat as well as fibre.

Drinks

Avoid all canned and bottled fizzy drinks except for the 'diet' or low-calorie versions.

Buy unsweetened fruit juices and add some carbonated mineral water to make your own fizzy drinks.

Try to avoid alcohol altogether while losing weight (see Chapter 10) although you can treat yourself to the occasional glass of wine.

Now you're ready to go!

BUT, before you set off make a list – this isn't just a reminder, it will also help you to avoid the temptations at the cakes counter, those irresistible treats that pile on the fat!

Impulse shopping is in fact the worst kind – you won't really know just how much fat or sugar you're buying and once you've taken it home it's usually too late.

Finally, make sure you're not hungry – shopping on an empty stomach almost guarantees that you will give in to a tempting snack on the way round!

CHAPTER 8

Meal planning and eating out

*B*y now, you will understand how this diet works – by eating as little fat and sugar as possible, making sure you get a proper daily intake of fibre and taking a reasonable amount of exercise, you will find that excess fat disappears gradually and permanently.

To achieve success you don't need to starve. That's not to say you can eat all day and still expect to lose weight – after all, even wholemeal bread and pasta eaten in excess will still make you fat!

This diet is about moderation. Sensible portions of the right foods at proper intervals will ensure that you start to reduce your reserves of fat.

Don't expect miracles either – the aim is not to lose 10lbs during the first week – we've already seen how bad this is for your system and how it's likely to fail in the long run.

You can expect to lose 1-2lbs a week on this diet after changing your eating habits. This will continue steadily until you become leaner and fitter.

The principle of this diet is that it is *not* just a slimming method – it is a beneficial change in eating habits that you should adopt for life.

The aim is to reduce your weight naturally to within the right limits for your height – this weight loss should be fat and not lean tissue or water. The benefits of this diet will also be seen in your general health, fitness and energy levels.

Let's begin the diet by looking at a typical day.

Breakfast

Breakfast is an important meal, it provides the energy that is necessary to start the day and see you through until lunchtime. Skipping breakfast won't help you slim – it's far more likely that you'll resort to snacks or chocolate bars to give you a mid-morning boost instead.

Ideally, breakfast should set you up with a good complex carbohydrate reserve to be gradually released as energy during the morning and a few suggestions are shown below:

      Medium bowl of sugar-free muesli
or Medium bowl of oatmeal porridge
or Medium bowl of sugar-free bran cereal
      all with skimmed or semi-skimmed milk.

PLUS a thick slice of toast, ideally wholemeal, thinly spread with low-fat margarine if necessary, and topped with one of the following:

i) Baked beans
ii) Marmite and sliced tomato
iii) Sliced button mushrooms sautéed in a little olive oil or stock, with herbs
iv) Low-sugar fruit preserve.

These are really only suggestions for providing high levels of carbohydrate and fibre whilst avoiding fat and sugar – there is no strict regime to follow and you don't have to eat both stages if you're satisfied with one! If you prefer two slices of toast and preserve instead of cereals, just go ahead.

Other sensible savoury suggestions would be grilled kipper (without butter!) and occasionally a rasher or two of grilled bacon or a poached or boiled egg.

The idea is not to feel deprived but to reduce your intake of fat and sugar to the lowest acceptable level.

Lunch

Your choice of lunch will depend to some extent on whether or not you work away from home and whether or not you're single or have a family to feed.

It will also depend on whether or not you're expected to provide a traditional Sunday roast!

For most people, on most days, a sandwich is probably enough. This should preferably be wholemeal bread, thinly spread with low-fat margarine, with a filling that as far as possible avoids fat and sugar.

The following fillings are the right sort of choice and with some of them, you won't really need margarine on the bread!

Lean chicken and salad with yoghurt dressing.

Smoked fish or crab with parsley and a squeeze of lemon.

Cottage cheese with fruit or prawns.

Half-fat cheese with sliced gherkins.

Lean ham with mustard and sliced tomato.

Marmite and cucumber.

Low-fat soft cheese with watercress.

Again, these are just suggestions, the choice is yours, bearing in mind the aim of avoiding fats and sugar.

Remember too, to avoid crisps and chocolate bars – follow your sandwich with a piece of fresh fruit.

If you are at home for lunch have soup and a wholemeal roll – you'll find some recipes in Chapter 9.

Alternatively, have one of the breakfast savouries such as mushrooms on toast or wholemeal pasta with a simple sauce and a salad.

Again, avoid ready-made desserts – get used to finishing a meal with fresh fruit instead.

If you are faced with cooking a traditional Sunday roast try to choose poultry or game instead of red meat, with baked potatoes and salad or steamed vegetables as an accompaniment.

For dessert, go for fresh fruit salad or one of the recipes in Chapter 9.

Evening meal

These days, this is often the main meal of the day for many people. If this is true for you, try not to eat too late – allow at least two hours before going to sleep because your digestion then slows down as well. That's why it's usually uncomfortable to sleep on a full stomach and why you still feel full the next morning. Give your stomach a chance to work and keep your digestion and your metabolism moving.

For evening meals, just remember the rule – eat as little fat and sugar as possible and keep up the fibre!

Typical meals could be:

Grilled or baked fish with steamed vegetables.

Grilled chicken (without skin), salad and baked potato.

Pasta with tomato sauce and side salad.

Low-fat casserole with steamed vegetables or brown rice.

Chinese stir-fry vegetables with prawns and brown rice.

Low-fat fish pie and steamed vegetables.

Chicken kebabs with wholemeal pitta bread and salad.

Stuffed marrow or green peppers.

Rabbit fricassée with baked potato and green beans.

Low-fat kedgeree.

Chicken or vegetable curry with brown rice.

The choice and variety is endless when you think about it!

In the next chapter, you will find a host of mouthwatering recipes for low fat/low sugar meals and most of them are excellent for entertaining at home.

This diet is not about starvation or boredom – use your imagination within the low fat/low sugar principle and adapt your favourite recipes to fit.

How about eating out?

If you're going out to a restaurant, apply the same principles that we've already discussed. Avoid deep-fried foods, red meats, cream sauces and fattening desserts. Instead, eat healthily.

Choose chicken, game, fish or shellfish and steamed vegetables or salad. Instead of chips and roast potatoes go for the boiled or baked versions.

Ask for your meat to be trimmed of fat, grilled without butter and served without rich cream sauces.

If you have a choice, opt for Chinese, Malaysian or Japanese restaurants – that way you can be sure of getting straightforward, fresh ingredients without too much hidden fat.

However, watch out for the Chinese love of sugar and batter in dishes like sweet and sour pork or prawn balls.

Choose simple stir-fried dishes such as chicken and green peppers in black bean sauce, steamed fish, crab with asparagus, chicken with bamboo shoots or seasonal vegetables.

Choose plain boiled rice as an accompaniment and finish with fruit rather than fritters for dessert.

Indian restaurants tend to pose more of a problem since many of their dishes are cooked in ghee, a form of clarified butter that's loaded with calories!

The safest choices are tandoori dishes such as chicken or prawns, without the creamy massala sauce, accompanied with salad and naan bread or paratha.

Alternatively, the 'sizzling' dishes cooked and served on a hot iron platter are relatively low in fat when compared to the richer sauces.

Again, choose plain rice rather than pilao which tends to be oily, or, better still, stick to chapatis and parathas.

Unfortunately, Indian vegetable dishes don't escape the ghee, the best choices are lentils (dahl), okra (bindi) and spinach (sag) with the least added fat content.

As for desserts, the Indians have a great love of sugar syrup, milk solids and batter and these are all best avoided – go for fresh fruit, if available, instead.

Italian food offers many options for healthy eating as well as a few danger zones.

Again, apply the principle of low fat/low sugar. For example, Italians make wonderful salads from chicken and seafood – just avoid the mayonnaise.

Pasta dishes and risottos are also fine when the sauces are based around tomatoes, onion and mushroom with perhaps chicken or shellfish, but without added cream. Remember though, to avoid sprinkling cheese on top!

Italian cuisine includes many wonderful grilled and baked fish dishes, with a chance to try something different such as red mullet or fresh sardines.

Grilled meats and stews are often fine but watch out for breadcrumb coatings and cream-based sauces.

Other danger areas are sausages and cheeses. These appear in many traditional dishes so read the menu carefully or ask for a full description.

Pizza of course is usually coated with cheese, but in a decent pizza house you will find the simple tomato, olive and anchovy or vegetarian styles to choose from. Proper pizza dough, by the way, has no added fats or sugar.

Desserts though are often laden with sugar, liqueurs and cream, but Italians do usually offer imaginative fruit salads and wonderful water-ices instead.

Greek cuisine is peasant-based and one of the healthiest diets in the world.

Meat is usually grilled or braised in tomato, herb and onion-based sauces. Fish is treated in much the same way.

Bread is usually made from roughly-refined flour, olive oil is the staple cooking fat and yoghurt is the Greek alternative to cream.

The only areas to avoid perhaps are doner kebabs. In this country they are usually an opportunity to use up scraps of meat and lots of fat in a giant form of 'sausage'.

Desserts are usually soaked in honey with an incredibly high sugar content so, again, opt for fresh fruit such as melon or figs instead.

Party Time!

This is usually a danger zone for dieters! With bowls of roasted nuts, crisps, cheesy snacks and cream dips it can almost be described as a health hazard as well!

Fortunately, these days people are becoming more conscious of what they eat so you are more likely to find celery, carrot or cucumber sticks. These of course, are the ones to choose.

You might also find grissini (bread sticks) or Twiglets. These contain around a quarter of the fat content of potato crisps or roasted nuts.

Alcohol is the other problem (see Chapter 10) not just because of the empty calories but because it stimulates the appetite and creates a craving for snacks.

The best approach is to eat something healthy before you go and then avoid the fattening snacks as much as you possibly can without upsetting your hosts!

CHAPTER 9

Clever cooking

We've already seen the basic principles behind this diet and the type of ingredients that you should be buying. This chapter deals with the right kind of preparation and cooking methods to keep fat and sugar to a minimum.

A number of recipe suggestions follow to get you started and these range from simple snacks, right through to gourmet meals. At the end of the book we have suggested some further sources of health-conscious recipes that you might like to try.

Otherwise, be adventurous. Try adapting your favourite dishes by using a little olive oil instead of lots of butter, substitute fromage frais for cream in sauces and casseroles, try a teaspoon of honey instead of a tablespoon of sugar, top desserts with yoghurt instead of cream – there are so many tasty ways to avoid fat and sugar.

Preparation and cooking

These are just general guidelines. There are many excellent books that show food preparation and cooking methods in detail and one or two are listed in our section on recommended further reading at the end of this book.

Basically, we are making a few suggestions here that will help to reduce fat and sugar and keep-up your fibre intake.

First, make sure you have a stock of basic ingredients such as wholemeal flour, beans, pulses, herbs and maybe low-sodium salt if you are at all concerned about blood pressure.

Then, aim to avoid processed and convenience items such as stock cubes, pickles and sauces. As we've seen, they are often high in fats, salt and added sugar. Recipes follow so that you can make your own and know exactly what you are eating.

Chances are, you already have a good stock of basic equipment. We've already suggested that you throw out the deep-fat fryer but, make a point of replacing it with a two-level steamer and a wok – unless you already have them – because these will help you in preparing healthy meals.

When preparing and cooking food, keep in mind the basic aims of reducing fat, avoiding sugar and maintaining high levels of fibre.

Meat and poultry

With all meat and poultry, trim off any visible fat before cooking. Poultry should also be skinned since this is where the fat is mostly found. For casseroles and stir-fries, skin the poultry first. In roasting and grilling leave the skin on and remove it just before serving.

Most methods of cooking meat, apart from frying and deep-frying, are perfectly acceptable, bearing in mind the aim of reducing fat.

When roasting and grilling, make sure the joint or pieces of meat are placed on a wire rack to allow the fat to drain off. If you plan to make gravy from the pan juices, allow them to settle for a few minutes before skimming off all the fat.

Make sure that you frequently baste the drier types of meat such as veal and game. Brush them with a little olive oil or vegetable oil while roasting but never with lard or dripping.

For stewing or braising, lightly dust the pieces of meat with seasoned flour and brown them quickly in hot olive or vegetable oil.

After cooking, allow the stew or casserole to stand for a minute or two so that any fat rises to the top. Skim off as much fat as possible with a spoon or small ladle and then draw a piece of paper towel over the surface to remove the rest.

Fish and shellfish

The aim in cooking fish is to avoid adding fat to a low-fat, nutritious item of food.

Preferred cooking methods are therefore grilling, poaching, steaming and oven-baking in foil.

The latter method gives particularly good results, since all the juices and flavours are retained in cooking.

Shellfish are usually boiled before being served (with the exception of oysters) and are therefore an excellent choice for a low-fat diet.

Again, the aim is to avoid adding fat – there is no need to deep-fry shellfish in batter – if anything, it disguises the true flavours.

Also avoid cream sauces with fish and garlic butter with prawns. If you happen to like garlic prawns, try them the Mediterranean way – that is with a touch of olive oil and finely chopped garlic on a hot griddle (or frying pan), served with a wedge of lemon it's simple, delicious and far less fattening.

Vegetables and pulses

Vegetables should be prepared immediately before cooking. They should be washed and, if necessary scrubbed with a brush to clean them.

Aim to remove as little peel as possible since the most nutritious part of potatoes, root vegetables and onions is just below the skin.

Never leave vegetables to soak before cooking since many nutrients are soluble in water – this is why steaming and microwaving are much healthier ways of cooking than boiling.

The exception to this is pulses, such as dried beans and lentils which need to be washed thoroughly, steeped in boiling water and left to soak for 2 hours or more.

They should then be boiled rapidly in fresh water, with a teaspoon of salt, for at least 10 minutes and left to simmer as follows: butter beans 2½-3 hours, haricot beans 2-2½ hours, kidney beans ½-¾ hour, peas 1-1½ hours, lentils ½-¾ hour. They can then be drained and used cold in salads or added to stews and casseroles.

When cooking vegetables, try to avoid overdoing them. Cook them to the point where they are tender but still firm – this ensures that the nutrients, the fibre and the flavours are all retained. If stir-fried they should still be crunchy.

Fruit

Fruit is at its best when fresh – it's the perfect way to end a meal. There's now such a variety available all year round, so be imaginative! Don't create a dull routine of apples, oranges and bananas.

Try cape gooseberries, dates, figs, kumquats, lychees, mangoes, passion fruit and pawpaws, to name but a few.

Also, try combining fruits in salads – some recipes follow later in this chapter.

Fruit can, of course, be cooked in several ways. It can be poached, stewed, baked or puréed and used in flans, whips, mousses and sorbets or served with meat or fish.

It's also the basis for low-sugar jams and chutneys - (recipes follow later).

Again, the same principle applies – as far as possible avoid adding fats and sugar.

Rice and pasta

We've looked at the benefits of choosing wholemeal pasta and brown rice (see Chapter 6 on fibre) and they should really be cooked as directed in the packet instructions.

Traditionally, many people add butter and ground black pepper to freshly cooked pasta in order to stop it congealing into a solid lump. However, if you add a teaspoon of olive oil to the cooking water and rinse the pasta with a dash of cold water when cooked it will stay perfectly separate without adding further oil or butter.

Brown rice is far easier to keep light and separate than the white varieties. It's difficult to overcook unless the suggested time is ridiculously exceeded so in fact it is much more likely to be a success in beginners' hands. Although it takes longer to cook, the flavour is far superior to white rice – especially the Basmati variety.

Another useful, natural grain is wild rice. Strictly speaking, it isn't a rice at all but the seed of an American native grass. Wild rice has an outstanding flavour and goes particularly well with game birds, poultry and shellfish.

Pastries and baking

Pastry is best avoided while you are trying to lose weight, but once you are down to a healthy level you can occasionally indulge in one of the types of pastry that are low in saturated fats and sugar.

The idea is to avoid butter, eggs and block margarine by selecting a safflower margarine that's high in polyunsaturates (beware of margarines containing palm and coconut oils, they are higher in saturated fats than butter!).

This means that simple, shortcrust pastries are your best bet (recipe suggestions follow). Choux pastry, puff pastry, flaky pastry and suet crusts are definitely fattening and should therefore be avoided.

The same applies to cakes and biscuits. The eggs, butter, milk and sugar required are totally at odds with your healthy new start.

When making pastry, don't forget to keep up the fibre – try to use wholemeal flour or at least a 50/50 mixture with white.

Recipe Section

Stocks

Stocks form the basis for soups, sauces and casseroles. Your own, home–made stock will be far superior to the slightly artificial and salty flavour of commercial stock cubes, as well as being virtually free of fat. The recipes all use 1 litre of water but may be doubled or trebled as you wish.

Vegetable Stock

1lb (450g) of vegetable trimmings
1 ¾ pints (1 litre) water
bouquet garni
6 peppercorns
½ teaspoon salt

Put all the ingredients together in a large pan, cover and bring to the boil. Reduce the heat and simmer for 1-2 hours. Strain the stock through a fine sieve or muslin and discard the vegetable matter.

Fish Stock

1 ½lb (675g) of cleaned, white fish trimmings such as bones, heads and skin (but not gills or entrails)
1 ¾ pints (1 litre) water
1 medium onion, finely chopped
bouquet garni
6 peppercorns

Put the fish and the water in a large pan and bring slowly to the boil, removing any surface scum with a spoon or ladle. Add the remaining ingredients and simmer, uncovered for 20-30 minutes. Strain the stock through a fine sieve or muslin and leave to cool.

Meat or game stock

1lb (450g) marrow bones, cracked or cut into pieces
1lb (450g) shin of beef or poultry or game bird carcass and giblets
1 ¾ pints (1 litre) of water
1 onion, sliced
1 leek, sliced
1 celery stalk, coarsely chopped
1 carrot, coarsely chopped
bouquet garni
6 peppercorns
1 clove garlic
½ teaspoon salt

Put the bones in a roasting pan and roast in an oven set at 230°C/Gas Mark 8 for 35-40 minutes, turning occasionally, until well-browned.

Transfer the bones to a large pan and add all the other ingredients. Bring slowly to the boil and remove any scum with a spoon or ladle, cover and simmer for about 4 hours, topping up the water if necessary to keep the ingredients covered.

Strain the stock through a fine sieve or muslin and leave to cool. Once cold, any fat will have set solid on the surface and can easily be lifted off with a spoon.

Italian Tomato Soup

Serves 4

2lbs (900g) large ripe tomatoes, peeled and coarsely chopped
2 medium onions, finely chopped
4 cloves garlic, chopped
1 heaped tablespoon of fresh basil or parsley
1 ½ pts (850ml) vegetable stock or water
2 tablespoons olive oil
1 level tablespoon plain flour
¼ pt (150ml) natural yoghurt
salt and pepper to taste

Heat the oil in a pan and gently fry the onions until soft. Sprinkle over the flour, and cook for a further 3 minutes, stirring continuously. Add the tomatoes, garlic and herbs and simmer until the tomatoes are soft and pulpy. Add the stock or water, bring to the boil, and simmer for another 20 minutes. Rub the soup through a coarse sieve, return to the boil and adjust seasoning. Remove from the heat and stir in the yoghurt. Serve with a garnish of freshly chopped parsley or basil.

Minestrone Soup

Serves 4

1 onion, chopped
1 leek, sliced
1 small cabbage, coarsely chopped
1 clove garlic, crushed
10oz (350g) cooked haricot beans (see page 44)
2pts (1 ¼ litres) chicken or vegetable stock
2 tablespoons olive oil
1 tablespoon chopped fresh basil or parsley
salt and pepper to taste

Sauté the onion and garlic in oil, in a large pan, until soft and slightly browned. Add the remaining ingredients, bring to the boil, cover and simmer for 25-30 minutes. Transfer about one quarter of the vegetables to a blender or food processor, purée them and then return the purée back to the pan. Return to the boil, simmer for 5 minutes and serve with a garnish of finely chopped parsley or basil.

Clockwise from top: Watercress and Almond; Italian Tomato; Cauliflower; Minestrone.

Watercress and Almond Soup Serves 6

1 tablespoon safflower oil
8 oz (225g) potatoes diced
2 bunches watercress
grated rind of 1 lemon
4 oz (100g) ground almonds
1 ½ pints (850 ml) chicken or vegetable stock
½ pint (300ml) semi-skimmed milk
salt and pepper

Heat the oil in a large, heavy-based pan and saute the potatoes, watercress and lemon rind for about one minute. Add the almonds, stock and milk and simmer for 20 minutes until cooked. Transfer to a food processor and blend until smooth. Return to the pan, re-heat and season to taste with salt and pepper. Garnish with sprigs of fresh watercress.

Cauliflower Soup Serves 6

1 medium cauliflower, cut into sprigs
1 large onion, sliced
2 cloves garlic, crushed
1 ¾ pints (1 litre) chicken stock
2 tablespoons olive oil
½ pint (300ml) semi-skimmed milk
salt and pepper to taste

Heat the oil in a large pan. Add the onion and garlic and cook gently until soft. Add the cauliflower and stock. Bring to the boil, cover and simmer gently for 1 hour. Pass the soup through a coarse sieve or purée in a blender. Return to the pan and re-heat to simmering point. Remove from the heat and stir in the milk. Serve with a garnish of freshly chopped parsley

Baked Trout with Fennel

Serves 6

6 rainbow trout, gutted and cleaned
1 bulb fennel, thinly sliced across the bulb
2 lemons
1 teaspoon safflower oil

Take a piece of baking foil large enough to loosely wrap the fish and place it centrally in a roasting tray. Lightly oil the foil and put the fennel slices down in a layer. Place the fish on top. Thinly grate the rind of one lemon and then extract the juice. Mix the rind and juice together and spread it over the fish. Wrap the foil into a loose parcel and place the tray in the centre of a pre-heated oven at 180°C/Gas Mark 4 for 20 minutes. Garnish with the fennel leaves or fresh dill and serve with lemon wedges.

Fish Pie

Serves 4

1lb (450g) of white fish (cod, haddock, hake or whiting)
1lb (450g) ripe tomatoes, skinned and chopped
1 large onion, chopped
1 clove garlic, crushed
1 green pepper, finely chopped
1 tablespoon chopped parsley
1 bay leaf
1 ½ lbs (675g) potatoes
¼ pt (150ml) semi-skimmed milk
2 tablespoons safflower oil
1 rounded teaspoon low-fat margarine
salt and black pepper

Poach the fish gently for 10 minutes with a dash of salt and pepper, in just enough water to cover it. Peel the potatoes and boil them for about 20 minutes or until well-cooked. Drain the potatoes and mash them thoroughly with the milk and margarine, season with black pepper.

Meanwhile, heat the oil in a frying pan and fry the onion and green pepper together until the onion is soft. Add the tomatoes, garlic, parsley and bay leaf and cook for a further 5 minutes – season to taste.

Lift the fish from its liquid, remove all skin and bones, flake the flesh and add it to the vegetable mixture. Remove the bay leaf and transfer the mixture to an ovenproof pie dish.

Cover the mixture evenly with the mashed potato, fork it smooth, and transfer the dish to a pre-heated oven 200°C/Gas Mark 6 for around 25 minutes until nicely browned.

Chinese-style Steamed Fish
Serves 4

2lb sea trout, bass, sea bream or large rainbow trout
1 tablespoon sesame oil
1 tablespoon light soy sauce
1 tablespoon dry sherry
4 cloves garlic, finely sliced
6 spring onions, shredded into 2" strands
2" (5cm) piece of root ginger, cut into fine strands
3 tablespoons water (or dry white wine)
1 teaspoon cornflour

Mix the oil, soy sauce and sherry together and brush some of the mixture all over the fish, inside and out. Mix the garlic, ginger and spring onions together and place half this mixture inside the fish. Gently curl the fish into the steamer or place it flat on a heatproof plate inside a wok.

Scatter the remaining garlic/ginger/onion mixture over the fish, cover tightly and steam vigorously for 15 – 20 minutes until the fish is tender.

Mix the remaining oil/soy sauce/sherry mixture with the wine or water and cornflour in a small saucepan. Bring to the boil and simmer for a minute or so, stirring continuously until the sauce thickens slightly. Lift the whole fish onto a serving plate and pour over the sauce. Serve with plain boiled or steamed rice and stir-fried vegetables (page 58).

Scampi Provencale
Serves 4

1lb (450g) large shelled prawns, cleaned and rinsed
1 onion, finely chopped
2 cloves garlic, finely chopped
14oz (400g) tin plum tomatoes, roughly chopped
3 tablespoons dry white wine
1 tablespoon olive oil
1 tablespoon chopped parsley
pinch of dried thyme
1 teaspoon cornflour
salt and pepper to taste

Heat the oil in a heavy-based pan and fry the onion gently until soft. Add the garlic and scampi and fry for a further 2-3 minutes. Stir in the tomatoes with the wine and seasonings, bring to the boil and simmer for 5 minutes or so.

Blend the cornflour with a dash of water and stir into the dish. Cook for another minute or two, stirring constantly, until the sauce has thickened.

Garnish with the chopped parsley and serve with plain boiled rice and green beans.

Beef Stroganoff

Serves 4

1lb (450g) fillet or rump steak
2 onions, finely chopped
4oz (100g) button mushrooms, sliced
1 tablespoon safflower oil
1 tablespoon tomato purée
7 fl ozs (200ml) beef stock
½ teaspoon ground nutmeg
1 level tablespoon cornflour
150g carton natural yoghurt
freshly ground black pepper

Cut the steak across the grain into ½" (12mm) thick slices, season with freshly-ground black pepper and flatten each slice with a wooden mallet or rolling pin.

Heat the oil in a frying pan and sauté the onion over a low heat until soft. Add the beef and sauté for about 5 minutes until browned. Using a slotted spoon, transfer the meat and onion to a heavy-based pan. Sauté the mushrooms in the juices left in the frying pan and add to the beef. Stir in the stock, tomato purée and nutmeg, bring to the boil, season to taste and simmer gently for 15 minutes. Mix the cornflour with a dash of water, add it to the pan and stir until thickened. Remove the pan from the heat, stir in the yoghurt and transfer to a serving dish. Serve with plain boiled rice and green beans or peas.

Chilli con Carne

Serves 6

1lb (450g) lean minced beef
12oz (350g) dried red kidney beans (cooked as directed on page 44) or 2 tins
2 onions, thinly sliced
14oz (400g) tin plum tomatoes, roughly chopped
1 tablespoon olive oil
2 teaspoons chilli powder (or finely chopped fresh chilli pepper)
½ teaspoon powdered cumin
salt and freshly ground black pepper to taste

Heat the oil in a heavy-based pan and fry the onions until soft. Add the meat and continue frying, stirring occasionally, until browned. Stir in the beans, the tomatoes and their juice, and all the seasonings.

Cover the pan with a tight fitting lid and simmer for 1-1½ hours, adding water if necessary to prevent drying out.

Serve with tossed green salad and plain boiled rice or warm crusty wholemeal bread.

Clockwise from top: Lamb Kebabs; Beef Stroganoff; Chilli con Carne; Fillet of Pork with Mushroom Sauce.

Meat dishes

1 lemon
salt and freshly ground black pepper

Trim any visible fat from the lamb and cut into 1" (25mm) cubes. Put the yoghurt into a large bowl and stir in the juice of half the lemon. Add all the other ingredients, including the lamb, and leave to marinate for at least one hour in a cool place.

Remove the cubes of lamb from the marinade and pack them tightly onto 4 metal skewers, cook under a hot grill, turning occasionally, for about 10 minutes.

Serve with hot, wholemeal pitta bread and a tossed green salad. Garnish with wedges of lemon and pickled green chilli peppers (if you like them!).

Fillet of Pork with Mushroom Sauce

1 ½lbs (675g) pork fillet   *Serves 6*
3 tablespoons safflower oil
1 tablespoon dry white wine
1 tablespoon lemon juice
8oz (200g) button mushrooms, thinly sliced
1 onion, finely chopped
2 tablespoons dry sherry
200g natural yoghurt
salt and freshly ground black pepper

Trim off any fat and sinew from the pork. Cut the meat across the grain into 2" (50mm) thick slices. Lay the slices between two sheets of dampened greaseproof paper and beat them flat with a mallet or rolling pin. Place the slices in a shallow dish.

Mix 2 tablespoons of safflower oil with the wine, lemon juice, garlic and black pepper. Pour this over the pork and leave for at least 2 hours in a cool place.

Heat 1 tablespoon of oil in a pan and fry the onion gently until soft. Add the mushrooms and fry for another 2-3 minutes. Lift the vegetables from the pan with a slotted spoon and keep them warm.

Drain the pork and discard the marinade. Fry gently, without adding further oil, for 3-4 minutes, turning once. Remove to a hot serving dish and keep warm.

Pour the sherry into the frying pan and heat briskly stirring constantly until reduced by half. Lower the heat and return the vegetables to the pan. Season to taste with salt and black pepper. Stir in the yoghurt and heat gently, stirring all the time, until the sauce almost reaches boiling point.

Pour the sauce over the pork and serve with brown Basmati or wild rice and green beans.

Lamb Kebabs   *Serves 4*

1 ½lbs (675g) lean lamb
150g carton natural yoghurt
1 green chilli pepper, finely chopped
1" (25mm) piece of root ginger, peeled and chopped
1 clove garlic, crushed
pinch of ground coriander

Lemon chicken

Serves 4

12oz (350g) chicken breasts, skinned and cut across the grain into ¼" (6mm) slices
1 onion, finely chopped
1 clove garlic, crushed
4oz (100g) button mushrooms, sliced
rind of 1 lemon, finely grated
juice of 1 lemon
4 tablespoons water
1 tablespoon light soy sauce
freshly ground black pepper
1 tablespoon safflower oil

Heat the oil in a wok or large frying pan. Cook the onion and garlic for 2 minutes, stirring frequently. Push the onion to one side and add the chicken pieces. Stir-fry for 2-3 minutes on high heat. Reduce heat and stir in the soy sauce and mushrooms – stir-fry for 1 minute, mixing in the onions and garlic. Add the lemon rind, lemon juice and water, bring to the boil and cook for 1 minute. Season with pepper to taste.

Serve with noodles and a tossed green salad.

Chicken Breasts in Tomato Sauce

Serves 4

12oz (350g) chicken breasts, skinned
14oz (400g) tin plum tomatoes, roughly chopped
1 onion, finely chopped
1 carrot, finely chopped
1 celery stalk, finely chopped
4oz (100g) lean ham, cut into thin strips
1 tablespoon olive oil
¼ pint (150ml) dry white wine
1 tablespoon chopped parsley
salt and black pepper

Lightly beat the chicken breasts with a mallet or rolling pin. Heat the oil in a large frying pan and cook the onion, carrot and celery until the onion is soft. Add the chicken breasts and cook for about 4 minutes, turning occasionally. Season to taste with salt and pepper. Add the wine and cook vigorously until it reduces by half. Stir in the tomatoes, ham and parsley and continue cooking for about 15 minutes, stirring occasionally, by which time the tomato sauce should have thickened.

Garnish with freshly chopped parsley and serve with brown rice.

Poultry dishes

Chinese Cashew Chicken

Serves 4

12oz (350g) chicken breasts, skinned and cut into ½" (12mm) cubes
2 tablespoons dry sherry
2 teaspoons cornflour
2 tablespoons of water
1-2 tablespoons safflower oil
4 spring onions, chopped into ½" (12mm) lengths
2 garlic cloves, finely chopped
1" (25mm) root ginger, peeled and cut into fine strips
1 tablespoon light soy sauce
4oz (100g) natural cashew nuts

Heat the oil in a wok or large frying pan. Stir fry the spring onions, garlic and ginger together for about 30 seconds. Add the chicken and stir-fry for another 2-3 minutes or until the flesh turns white. Mix the cornflour with the water and add it to the pan along with the sherry and the soy sauce. Stir well, add the cashew nuts and cook for a minute, stirring constantly.

Serve with steamed or boiled rice and stir-fried vegetables (page 58).

Turkey Escalopes in Mustard Sauce

4 turkey escalopes *Serves 4*
2 leeks cut into fine (julienne) strips
2 carrots cut into fine (julienne) strips
2 courgettes cut into fine (julienne) strips
2 celery stalks cut into fine (julienne) strips
1 tablespoon safflower oil
8fl oz (250ml) white wine
200g natural yoghurt
1 tablespoon Dijon mustard
salt and black pepper

Steam the vegetables for about 5 minutes until just tender but still firm.

Heat the oil in a frying pan. Sprinkle the escalopes with a little salt and freshly ground black pepper to taste. Sauté the escalopes for 4-5 minutes on each side, turning once.

Remove the escalopes from the pan and keep warm. Remove any excess oil from the pan. Add the wine and boil, stirring occasionally, until reduced by half. Stir in the yoghurt and mustard and heat until almost boiling, then stir in the vegetables.

Serve the escalopes on individual plates and spoon over the sauce. Accompany with baked or mashed potatoes.

Rabbit with Prunes

Serves 4

1 rabbit, 2 ¼lb (1kg) cut into 6-8 neat joints
6oz (175g) prunes
1 onion, chopped
1-2 tablespoons olive oil
8fl oz (250ml) red wine
8fl oz (250ml) game or poultry stock
1 clove garlic, crushed
½ teaspoon dried thyme
½ teaspoon dried rosemary
2 bay leaves
1 tablespoon parsley, chopped
salt and black pepper

Pour boiling water over the prunes and soak until cool. Heat the oil in a large, heavy-based pan or casserole dish and cook the rabbit pieces until browned all over. Add the onion and cook until lightly browned.

Stir in the wine, rosemary, thyme and bay leaves and bring to the boil. Add the stock, garlic and salt and pepper to taste. Return to the boil, cover and simmer for one hour. Drain the prunes, add them to the dish, cover and simmer for a further 15 minutes or until the rabbit is tender.

Transfer the rabbit pieces to a serving dish and pour the prunes on top. Reduce the sauce by boiling (until it just coats a spoon) and pour over the rabbit and prunes. Garnish with chopped parsley and serve with baked potatoes.

Pigeon with Cherries

Serves 4

2 plump, young pigeons, halved
1 tablespoon olive oil
2 tablespoons dry sherry
1 clove garlic, crushed
14oz (400g) can black cherries, drained
½oz (12g) cornflour
1 dessertspoon tomato purée
½pt (300ml) game or poultry stock
2 bay leaves
salt and black pepper
1 bunch watercress

Heat the oil in a large heavy-based pan and brown the pigeon halves, turning once. Add the garlic, pour over the sherry and cook for a few moments. Remove from the heat and transfer the pigeons to a warm dish. Blend the cornflour and tomato purée with a little stock and stir into the pan with the garlic and sherry.

Clockwise from top: Salmis of Venison; Pigeon with Cherries; Rabbit with Prunes; Normandy-style Pheasant;

Add the remaining stock gradually, stirring constantly, and bring to the boil. Simmer until the sauce thickens, stirring well. Return the pigeons to the pan, add the bayleaves and salt and pepper to taste. Cover with foil and simmer gently for 1½–2 hours until the birds are tender. Add the cherries about 10 minutes before the end of the cooking time. Serve on individual plates, garnished with watercress.

Game dishes

Mix the marinade ingredients together in a flat dish and marinate the venison for 6-8 hours in a cool place, stirring occasionally.

Drain the meat thoroughly and pat dry with kitchen towel. Reserve the marinade. Heat the fresh oil in a large pan and fry the onion until soft. Add the venison and brown all over. Sprinkle lightly with flour and stir the meat and onion until well coated.

Add the wine, garlic and bouquet garni and cover the pan with a lid. Cook gently for about 1 hour and then add the strained marinade. Continue cooking for a further hour or so until the meat is really tender. Remove the bouquet garni and check the seasoning with salt and freshly ground black pepper. Allow the dish to stand for a minute or two and skim off any surface fat.

Normandy-style Pheasant   Serves 6

2 pheasants
1½lbs (675g) Cox's or aromatic eating apples, peeled, cored and cut into wedges
1 tablespoon olive oil
1 tablespoon safflower oil
¼ teaspoon cinnamon
¼pt (150ml) dry cider
¼pt (150ml) game or chicken stock
salt and black pepper

Preheat the oven to 200°C/Gas Mark 6. Trim any visible yellow fat from the pheasants and season them inside and out with salt and pepper.

Sauté the apples in a frying pan with safflower oil and cinnamon until lightly browned. Transfer them to a deep casserole that will hold the two birds snugly.

Wipe the frying pan, heat the olive oil and brown the pheasants on all sides. Place the pheasants, breast down, on top of the apples. Add the cider and stock to the juices left in the frying pan and heat to boiling point, stirring well. Pour the stock over the pheasants, cover the casserole and transfer it to the oven. After 20 minutes turn the pheasants over onto their backs and return to the oven for a further 30 minutes until cooked through. Transfer the pheasants to a carving dish and keep warm.

Sieve the apples and juices into a saucepan and boil vigorously until they reach an apple sauce consistency. Allow the sauce to stand for a minute or two, skim off any surface fat and check the seasoning.

Carve the pheasants and serve the sauce separately in a warm jug.

Salmis of Venison   Serves 4

2lbs (900g) venison, cut into 1" cubes
1–2 tablespoons olive oil
2 onions, chopped
½pt (300ml) red wine
2 garlic cloves, crushed
bouquet garni
salt and black pepper
flour for dusting

Marinade
1 onion, finely chopped
3 tablespoons olive oil
2 tablespoons red wine
1 bay leaf
sprig of rosemary
sprig of thyme
pinch of salt
6 black peppercorns

Chinese stir-fried vegetables

Serves 6

1½lbs (750g) prepared vegetables such as Chinese leaf, leeks, button mushrooms, spring onions, green beans, mangetout peas or cauliflower in any combination
2 tablespoons safflower oil
1 clove garlic, crushed
1 teaspoon freshly grated ginger
4fl oz (100ml) vegetable stock or water
1 tablespoon oyster sauce
1 tablespoon light soy sauce
2 teaspoons cornflour

Cut the Chinese leaf, leeks, beans or spring onions across the grain into 1½" (38mm) slices. Break cauliflower into florets, slice mushrooms thickly, leave mangetout peas whole.

Heat the oil in a wok or deep frying pan with the garlic and ginger. Add the vegetables and stir-fry for 2 minutes. Mix the sauces and stock (or water) together and add to the pan. Cover and simmer well for 4 minutes. Mix the cornflour with a little cold water. Push the vegetables to one side and stir in the cornflour to the stock. Return to the heat and stir the dish constantly until the sauce thickens.

Serve immediately with boiled rice, or as an accompaniment to other Chinese-style dishes.

Stuffed Green Peppers

Serves 4

4 green peppers
2 tablespoons olive oil
4oz (100g) brown rice
1 small onion, chopped
2oz (50g) mushrooms, chopped
thick slice lean ham, finely diced (optional)
1 tablespoon pine nuts, chopped
2 tablespoons tomato purée
¾pt (450ml) chicken or vegetable stock
1 tablespoon chopped parsley
salt and black pepper

Slice the top off each pepper and reserve. Remove all pith and seeds. Steep the peppers in boiling water and leave to stand for 5 minutes. Drain well and dry.

Heat 1 tablespoon of oil in a heavy-based pan and sauté the rice for a few minutes until golden. Cover with two-thirds of the stock and bring to the boil, stirring constantly. Reduce the heat, cover and simmer for about 30 minutes adding a little more stock if necessary to prevent drying out. Sauté the onions, mushrooms and pine nuts in 1 tablespoon of oil, drain well and add to the rice. Stir–in the ham and parsley, season to taste, and fill each pepper with the mixture.

Arrange the peppers in a flat, oven–proof dish, and replace the caps. Blend the tomato purée with the remaining stock and pour over the peppers. Transfer the dish to a pre–heated oven at 180°C/Gas Mark 4 and bake for 35–40 minutes, or until done, basting frequently. Garnish with chopped parsley.

Vegetable dishes

2 tablespoons chopped parsley
1 bay leaf
salt and black pepper

Heat the oil in a large, heavy-based pan and fry the garlic, onion, carrot and celery until softened. Add the remaining ingredients, season to taste, cover and simmer for about 1 hour, stirring occasionally, until the lentils are tender but not too mushy.

Garnish with chopped parsley and serve with hot, crusty wholemeal bread or rolls.

Stuffed Vine Leaves (Dolmas)   Serves 4

12 fresh vine or young cabbage leaves
4oz (100g) brown rice
1 onion, finely chopped
2 tablespoons pine nuts, chopped
1½pts (900ml) chicken or vegetable stock
1 tablespoon chopped parsley
1 level teaspoon mixed dried herbs
juice of half lemon
1-2 tablespoons olive oil
200g natural yoghurt
1 tablespoon finely chopped mint
salt and black pepper

Heat the oil in a large, heavy-based pan and sauté the rice, pine nuts and onion until lightly browned. Add sufficient stock to cover the rice, bring to the boil and simmer until the rice is cooked. Stir frequently and add further stock as necessary to prevent drying out. Once cooked, allow the rice to cool and set. Then, stir in the herbs and parsley and season with salt and pepper to taste.

Blanch the vine or cabbage leaves in boiling water for 3-4 minutes and remove any coarse stalks.

Spread the leaves out flat and put a tablespoon of rice mixture into the centre of each one. Fold the sides of each leaf over the filling, turn over the bottom edge and roll away from you to form a neat, cylindrical parcel.

Pack the parcels closely, in layers if necessary, in a flameproof casserole dish. Add enough stock to cover and pour over the lemon juice. Put a plate over the parcels to keep them submerged, cover the dish and simmer gently for 1 hour. Lift the parcels out with a slotted spoon and serve hot or cold with wholemeal pitta bread and the natural yoghurt with chopped mint stirred in.

Lentil Stew   Serves 4-6

1–2 tablespoons safflower oil
2 onions, chopped
4 carrots, sliced
4 celery sticks, sliced
2 cloves garlic, crushed
1lb (500g) ripe tomatoes, skinned and chopped
10oz (300g) lentils, soaked (page 44)
½pt (300ml) tomato juice
1½ pts (900ml) vegetable stock

Three Bean Salad

Serves 6

6oz (170g) butter beans
6oz (170g) red kidney beans
6oz (170g) haricot beans
6 spring onions, in thick slices
4 tablespoons French dressing
3 tablespoons chopped parsley

Cook the beans as shown on page 44 and drain. While still warm, mix in the onions and dressing. Allow to cool and stir in the parsley before serving.

Waldorf Salad

Serves 6

1lb (450g) red dessert apples, cored and diced
½ head of celery, thinly sliced
2oz (50g) walnuts, roughly chopped
200g natural yoghurt
2 tablespoons lemon juice
1 lettuce

Stir the apple into the lemon juice and allow to stand for 5 minutes. Add the celery, walnuts and yoghurt, mix well, and serve in the centre of a bowl lined with lettuce leaves.

If you wish, you can add ¾lb (350g) of diced, cooked chicken to create Chicken Waldorf, a meal in itself!

Cracked Wheat Salad

Serves 6

4oz (100g) cracked (Bulgar) wheat
¼ cucumber, cut in ¼" (6mm) cubes
4 ripe tomatoes, skinned, seeded and roughly chopped
4 spring onions, finely chopped
2 tablespoons natural yoghurt
juice of 1 lemon
1 tablespoon finely chopped mint
black pepper

Soak the wheat in plenty of cold water for 30-40 minutes (or as directed). Drain in a sieve and press down with a spoon to squeeze out any excess water.

Mix all the ingredients in a serving bowl and season to taste with black pepper.

Clockwise from top left: Winter Coleslaw; Three Bean Salad; Waldorf Salad; Cracked Wheat Salad.

Winter Coleslaw

Serves 6

½ small white cabbage, shredded
2 large carrots, grated
3 sticks celery, finely chopped
1 dessert apple, diced
2oz (50g) sultanas
2oz (50g) walnuts, chopped
juice of half lemon
200g natural yoghurt
salt and black pepper to taste

Place all the ingredients in a salad bowl, toss thoroughly and chill before serving.

An ideal accompaniment to cold meat and baked potato.

French Dressing

6fl oz (175ml) olive or walnut oil
2 tablespoons white wine vinegar
2 tablespoons lemon juice
1 clove garlic, crushed
½ teaspoon mustard powder
salt and pepper to taste

Put all the ingredients in a screw-top bottle or jar and shake vigorously before serving.

Yoghurt Dressing

10oz (300g) natural yoghurt
2 tablespoons lemon juice
1 clove garlic, crushed
1 tablespoon mint, finely chopped
salt and pepper to taste

Mix all the ingredients together in a bowl and serve. Store in a refrigerator.

Soy and Oil Dressing

6fl oz (175 ml) olive oil
4 tablespoons soy sauce
2 tablespoons lemon juice
1 clove garlic, crushed
½ teaspoon powdered ginger
salt and pepper to taste

Put all the ingredients in a screw-top bottle or jar and shake vigorously before serving.

Bolognese Sauce (Ragù)

Serves 6

1-2 tablespoons olive oil
1 onion, finely chopped
1 carrot, finely chopped
1 celery stalk, finely chopped
2 cloves garlic, finely chopped
1lb (450g) lean minced beef
½lb (225g) ripe or tinned tomatoes, peeled and chopped
¼ pt (150 ml) beef stock
2 tablespoons red wine
1 teaspoon dried mixed herbs (oregano/thyme/basil)
1 bay leaf
Salt and black pepper to taste

Heat the oil in a large frying pan and cook the onion, garlic, carrot and celery until the onion softens.

Add the beef and continue frying until it browns. Add the wine and cook for a few minutes until it almost evaporates. Stir in the remaining ingredients and cook gently for about 1 hour, until the meat is soft. Stir occasionally and add a little stock or water if necessary.

Serve with spaghetti or noodles.

Mushroom Sauce

Serves 6

8oz (225g) mushrooms, thinly sliced
1 large onion, finely chopped
1-2 tablespoons olive oil
2 cloves garlic, finely chopped
6oz (170g) tomatoes, peeled and chopped
7 fl oz (200ml) beef stock
2 tablespoons red wine
1 tablespoon chopped parsley
salt and black pepper

Heat the oil in a large frying pan and cook the onion and garlic until soft. Add the mushrooms and cook for a further 2-3 minutes. Add the wine and cook until it is reduced by half. Add the stock and tomatoes and cook for 15-20 minutes. Season with salt and pepper to taste, stir in the parsley and cook gently for a further 10 minutes.

Serve with spaghetti or noodles.

Clockwise from top left: Marinara Sauce; Mushroom Sauce; Chicken Pilaf; Bolognese Sauce.

Rice and pasta

Marinara Sauce

Serves 6

1 onion, finely chopped
2 cloves garlic, finely chopped
1-2 tablespoons olive oil
1lb (450g) ripe tomatoes, skinned and chopped
1lb (450g) prawns, chopped if large
¼pt (150ml) dry white wine
3 tablespoons parsley, finely chopped
1 teaspoon dried herbs (oregano, basil or marjoram)
salt and black pepper

Sauté the onion and garlic in the olive oil until transparent. Add the tomatoes and dried herbs and simmer for 15-20 minutes. In a separate pan, simmer the prawns gently in the white wine for 5 minutes and then transfer this to the tomato sauce. Add the parsley, season with salt and pepper to taste, and simmer for 10 minutes.

Serve with spaghetti or tagliatelle.

Chicken Pilaf

Serves 6

¾lb (350g) cooked chicken, cut in small chunks
2 onions, finely chopped
2 cloves garlic, finely chopped
1-2 tablespoons olive oil
10oz (275g) long grain rice
1½pts (900ml) chicken stock
8oz (225g) button mushrooms, chopped
3 ripe tomatoes, skinned and chopped
½ teaspoon powdered saffron or cumin
salt and black pepper

Heat the oil in a large, flameproof casserole dish and fry the onion and garlic until soft. Add the rice and continue frying until it becomes transparent. Pour over the stock, add the mushrooms and saffron, season with salt and black pepper. Stir thoroughly, cover the dish and place it in the centre of a pre-heated oven 180°C/Gas Mark 4 for 40 minutes.

Remove the dish from the oven, stir-in the chicken pieces and return to the oven for a further 20 minutes until the rice has absorbed all the liquid.

Add a little extra stock if the rice dries up too quickly – the finished dish should be slightly moist.

Serve with a tossed green salad.

Dried Fruits Salad

Serves 6

6oz (175g) dried apricots
4oz (125g) dried prunes
4oz (125g) dried figs
4oz (125g) dried apples
1pt (600ml) apple juice
1oz (25g) chopped almonds or walnuts

Soak the fruit overnight in the apple juice. Transfer to a saucepan and simmer for 15 minutes or until the fruits are tender. Pour into a serving bowl and sprinkle over the chopped nuts.

Serve hot or cold with natural yoghurt.

Fruit Whip

Serves 6

1lb (450g) prepared soft fruit such as raspberries, strawberries, rhubarb, blackberries or gooseberries
2 teaspoons clear honey
1 tablespoon water
400g natural yoghurt
2 egg whites

Simmer the fruit with water and honey until soft (about 5-7 minutes). Purée through a coarse sieve or in a food processor. Leave to cool and then mix in a large bowl with the yoghurt. Chill for at least 30 minutes. Whisk the egg whites stiffly and fold them into the fruit and yoghurt just before serving.

Spoon into individual bowls and garnish with mint leaves and a piece of the fresh fruit if appropriate.

Canned fruits may be substituted, although the juice should be drained off.

Clockwise from top right: Baked Apples; Raspberry Sorbet; Dried Fruits Salad; Fruit Whip.

Raspberry Sorbet

8oz (225g) raspberries
1-2oz (25-50g) caster sugar
300g natural yoghurt
4 tablespoons water
juice of half lemon
½oz (14g) powdered gelatine
2 egg whites

Rub the raspberries through a sieve to make a thick purée. Sweeten to taste (the less sugar the better!). Stir in the yoghurt and lemon juice and keep chilled.

Put the water in a bowl and sprinkle over the gelatine. Leave to stand for 5 minutes and then place the bowl in a pan of hot water. Stir until the gelatine is completely dissolved and then add it to the raspberries and yoghurt.

Beat the egg whites until stiff and fold them into the purée. Transfer the mix to a plastic bowl, cover with a lid and place in the freezing compartment of the refrigerator (at the coldest setting). When almost frozen, remove the bowl from the freezer and whisk the purée until it becomes slushy. Return to the freezer until firmly set. Scoop into individual bowls and garnish with mint and a fresh raspberry.

Baked Apples   Serves 6

6 large cooking apples, washed and cored
1 tablespoon clear honey
4oz (100g) chopped, sweet dried fruit, such as
sultanas or figs
1 tablespoon lemon juice
1 tablespoon apple juice

Place the apples on an ovenproof dish. Heat the other ingredients in a small pan until the fruit has softened. Fill the apples with the fruit and pour over the remaining juices. Bake in a pre-heated oven 180°C/Gas Mark 4 for about 50 minutes until the apples are soft. Serve with a topping of natural yoghurt.

Pizza Siciliana

Serves 4-6

1oz (25g) dried yeast
8 fl oz (240ml) warm water
1lb (450g) plain flour (white and wholemeal)
1 teaspoon salt
1lb (450g) fresh ripe or tinned tomatoes, peeled and chopped
8 anchovy fillets
10-12 black olives, pitted and chopped
olive oil
1 teaspoon dried oregano or basil

Mix the yeast and warm water in a basin, stirring until dissolved. Add sufficient flour to make a soft, pliable dough. Cover and leave in a warm place to rise (approx 30 minutes). Mix the remaining flour and salt in a large bowl and make a well in the middle. Place the risen yeast into the well and mix together until the dough is firm enough to be gathered into a ball. Place on a floured board and knead vigorously for 15 minutes (this can be done with an electric mixer or food processor if preferred).

Once kneaded, shape the dough into a ball and put it in a large bowl. Cover with a damp cloth and leave in a warm place until doubled in size (about 1½ hours).

Once risen, roll out the dough and place it in the centre of an oiled baking tray (12in x 14in / 30 x 35cm) or pizza plate (14in / 35cm dia). Stretch and pull the dough until it reaches the edges of the tray (it should be no more than ¼in/6mm thick, except at the edges which may be twice as thick). Make light depressions all over the base with your fingers and brush lightly with olive oil.

Spread the tomatoes and olives over the base, almost to the edges, and arrange the anchovy fillets on top. Sprinkle with the herbs and a little olive oil and bake for 10 minutes in a pre-heated oven 240°C/Gas Mark 9.

Reduce the heat to 180°C/Gas Mark 4 and bake for a further 5-10 minutes until the edges are brown and crisp.

Sweet Pepper Flan

Serves 4-6

2oz (50g) polyunsaturated margarine
4oz (100g) wholemeal flour
2 tablespoons water
3 peppers (red, green or yellow in any combination)
1 large onion, finely chopped
1 clove garlic, finely chopped
1 tablespoon olive or safflower oil
2 ripe tomatoes, skinned and chopped
1 tablespoon tomato purée
3fl oz (85ml) water or dry white wine
salt and pepper

Mix the flour and a pinch of salt in a wide bowl. Rub in the margarine and add enough cold water to make a firm dough. Turn this onto a floured surface, roll out into a circle, and use to line an 8in (20cm) flan dish. Bake blind in a pre-heated oven 190°C/Gas Mark 5 for 20–25 minutes until lightly browned.

Flans and pastries

Date and Nut Scones   Makes 12-14

8oz (250g) wholemeal flour
½ teaspoon salt
½ teaspoon ground cinnamon
3 level teaspoons baking powder
2oz (50g) polyunsaturated margarine
1 tablespoon brown sugar
1oz (25g) dates, chopped
1oz (25g) walnuts, chopped
5oz (15g) natural yoghurt
sesame seeds

Mix the flour and salt in a bowl and sift-in the cinnamon and baking powder. Rub in the margarine until the mixture has an even, crumbly texture. Stir in the sugar, dates and walnuts followed by the yoghurt, and mix into a soft dough. Knead the dough lightly on a floured surface and roll out to ¾ inch (2cm) thickness. Cut into rounds using a 2 inch (5cm) fluted cutter and place on a floured baking sheet. Brush the tops with semi-skimmed milk and sprinkle over some sesame seeds. Bake in a pre-heated oven 220°C/Gas Mark 7 for 12-15 minutes. Allow to cool on a wire rack.

Apple Pie   Serves 4-6

4oz (125g) wholemeal flour
2oz polyunsaturated margarine
1-2 tablespoons cold water
1½lb (675g) dessert apples, peeled, cored and sliced
3 tablespoons apple or orange juice
¼ tsp powdered cinnamon and 2-3 cloves

Prepare the shortcrust pastry by mixing the flour and a pinch of salt in a wide bowl and rubbing in the margarine until a crumb-like consistency is obtained. Sprinkle the water evenly over the surface and mix the dough lightly with a round-bladed knife until large lumps are formed. Gather the dough with your fingers until it leaves the sides of the bowl clean. Roll it into a ball and knead it lightly on a floured surface until firm. Chill for 20-30 minutes.

Place a pie funnel in the centre of a 1½pt (900ml) pie dish. Arrange half of the apple slices in the bottom of the dish. Sprinkle with cinnamon and cloves, add the remaining apple slices and the juice. Cover the dish with the rolled-out pastry, decorate as required, brush the top with semi-skimmed milk and lightly dust with caster sugar. Make a slit in the centre of the pastry and place the dish on a baking tray in the centre of a pre-heated oven 200°C/Gas Mark 6 for 30-40 minutes until nicely browned.

Meanwhile, wash the peppers, remove the stalks and seeds and slice thinly. Sauté the onion and garlic in olive oil until soft and slightly golden. Add the tomatoes, purée and water or wine and simmer for 5 minutes. Add the peppers, season to taste with salt and black pepper, cover the pan and continue cooking for another 30 minutes until the peppers are tender and the liquid has almost evaporated away. Pour into the flan case and serve hot with a tossed green salad.

Jams and preserves

Low-sugar Tomato Ketchup
(5.5% added sugar)

6lbs (2.7kg) ripe tomatoes, quartered
6oz (175g) sugar
½ pt (300ml) spiced vinegar
1 teaspoon paprika
2 teaspoons salt
pinch of cayenne pepper

Gently cook the tomatoes in a large pan until the juices run. Increase the heat and boil vigorously until they reduce to a pulp; rub through a fine plastic sieve and place the purée in a clean pan. Add the remaining ingredients and bring to the boil, stirring frequently. Continue cooking until a sauce-like consistency is reached.

Pour the sauce into warm screw-cap bottles or preserving jars and seal. Process for 30 minutes by standing the jars on a trivet in a deep pan. Fill with water to 1" below the tops, bring to simmering point and simmer for 20 minutes, lift out the bottles or jars, tighten the caps and leave to cool.

Low-sugar Jam
(25% added sugar)

2lbs (900g) ripe soft fruit
juice of half lemon
11oz (300g) jam sugar (with added pectin)
⅓pt (200ml) water

Clean the fruit and remove any stones (if you are using apricots, peaches, plums or greengages, crack open 8 of the stones and blanch the kernels in boiling water for 5 minutes, peel and halve them and add them to the fruit which should be cut into quarters).

Put the fruit, water and lemon juice into a pan and simmer, until the fruit is pulpy. Stir in the sugar until it dissolves and bring to a rapid boil. Boil as directed on the sugar packet – this may only be 4 minutes – and transfer the jam to clean, warm jars. Seal immediately and store in a cool dark place. For longer term storage use vacuum seal jars with screw-on lids.

This type of jam does not set solid and will remain soft. Once opened, it should be stored in a refrigerator and used within one month.

'No-sugar' Jam
(no added sugar)

1lb (450g) soft, well-rippened fruit or soaked dried fruit
juice of half lemon
½oz (15g) gelatine
5 tablespoons water

Clean and prepare the fruit and put it in a pan with the lemon juice and 2 tablespoons of water. Simmer until the fruit is pulpy.

If using dried fruit, reduce it to pulp in a food processor. Dissolve the gelatine in 3 tablespoons of water and stir it into the fruit. Put it into a clean, warm jar and seal immediately.

Refrigerate when cool and use within one week.

Low-sugar Chutney
(10% added sugar)

1pt (600ml) malt vinegar
1lb (450g) apples, peeled, cored and sliced
½lb (225g) onions, peeled and chopped
½lb (225g) seedless raisins, chopped
1 teaspoon salt
2 teaspoons ground ginger
1 teaspoon mustard powder
1 teaspoon cayenne pepper
2 cloves garlic, finely chopped
4oz (100g) soft brown sugar

Cook the apples, onions and garlic with half the vinegar in a stainless steel pan until thick and pulpy. Add the remaining ingredients and vinegar and continue cooking for a further 20 minutes or so, until thick. Pot and cover with vinegar-proof tops. Leave 2 to 3 months before using.

CHAPTER 10

Booze and blubber

*M*ost slimming diets, including the fads, advise that alcoholic drinks should be avoided completely or reduced to the occasional glass of wine.

In this respect they are right.

Alcohol is in many ways the same as sugar – after all, along with yeast, that's what it's made of!

Alcoholic drinks contain little or no nourishment and merely supply empty calories – the kind of energy that tends to be stored as fat.

Alcohol, in excess, is also associated with many disorders and diseases apart from the obvious cirrhosis of the liver.

However, this diet is about moderation and enjoyment. If you enjoy the occasional drink there is probably no harm in a glass or two of wine each day so why add another area of self-denial when you are already making major changes to the way you eat?

In fact, some expert medical opinion suggests that a modest amount of alcohol may be beneficial in protecting against heart disease.

However, this whole area is very controversial in medical terms and the actual 'permitted' level is quite small – about 1½ pints of beer or 2-3 glasses of wine a day.

Another problem is that alcoholic drinks tend to stimulate the appetite – hence the traditional pre-dinner drinks – and therefore encourage you to eat more than you need. Alcohol also reduces your willpower and self-control.

On balance it is wise to restrict your intake of alcohol to within the level suggested above and avoid the drinks that are high in calories (sugar).

The table below shows the calorie content of a wide range of drinks and it is best to keep your intake down to no more than 200 calories a day.

BEER	*Calories per pint*
Bitter	192
Mild	150
Brown Ale	168
Pale Ale	192
Stout	228
Lager	174

WINE	*Calories per glass (100ml)*
Dry white	66
Champagne	76
Medium white	75
Sweet white	94
Red	68
Sweet Sherry	136
Dry Sherry	116
Port	157

CIDER	*Calories per pint*
Dry	216
Sweet	252
Vintage	606

SPIRITS	*Calories per measure (1.5fl oz)*
Brandy	100
Others	105

LIQUEURS	*Calories per fl oz*
Advocaat	82
Benedictine	75
Chartreuse	75
Curaçao	93
Cherry Brandy	76
Creme de menthe	90
Drambuie	65

CHAPTER 11

Exercise – is it worth the effort?

*F*or some of us, even the thought of taking exercise is too much to bear. However, taking exercise does not have to be the same as doing exercises.

We have already seen that every kind of physical activity throughout the day requires energy – from walking downstairs to making love – and the more energy you can use up, the less there will be left over to store as fat!

The trouble is, that with today's lifestyle, it is really easy to avoid a great deal of activity. Automation and labour-saving devices now replace much of the physical effort that would have been required in days gone by.

If you look back to the 1950's and beyond, most people walked or cycled to the shops or to visit friends. Washing and other household chores were done by hand as were gardening and DIY tasks.

Nowadays, we travel to work by car, bus or train. When we arrive, many of us are involved in work that keeps us sitting down for most of the time. When we go shopping, or to visit friends, how many of us walk or cycle these days?

This partly explains why levels of obesity and heart disease have increased so dramatically in recent generations.

"Do I really have to do exercises?"

You will probably be relived to know that the answer is not to rush out, buy a leotard and get down to the nearest aerobics class.

For a start, the sudden, extra demands on your body could be dangerous, especially if you are substantially overweight.

The important thing is to find a type of exercise that you can happily maintain as part of your life, not just a get-slim-quick type of punishment that you will really hate in a few weeks time.

Perhaps you can think back to a sport or activity that you once enjoyed. Swimming, cycling and tennis for example, are all excellent forms of exercise and it really doesn't matter how good you are unless you're looking to break records or play for your county!

Just 20 minutes or so, two or three times a week, is enough to get your system going and help to shed those extra pounds. Ideally, you should aim to build-up over a period of time to at least 30 minutes, three times a week.

"But I haven't got time for sports!"

Is time really the problem? After all we can all 'make' time to watch a regular TV programme or go to the pub on a particular evening. The answer is to find an activity that will become an enjoyable 'habit', then you will be quite surprised how quickly you 'find' the time to do it.

Be adventurous. Try something new. Your local sports centre will undoubtedly offer a wide range of activities for all ages and levels of physical fitness.

You don't necessarily have to try judo or karate. Maybe badminton, bowls or basketball would be more suited to your lifestyle.

Alternatively, look outside. Have you ever wanted to play golf, go sailing, horse riding or rambling through the countryside?

There are usually local groups or organisations that cater for every kind of activity. Don't be afraid to ask – people are always glad to share their particular interest with newcomers.

If you find something you enjoy, the benefits are enormous. Not only do you get the extra level of activity to bring your weight down but you will also benefit from greater fitness, less stress and a chance to make new friends.

"Are there easier ways to exercise?"

If you really can't manage an hour or two of sport each week on a regular basis then do think carefully about doing some simple exercises at home.

You will find the following routines easy to start – they don't require too much effort so you can start exercising gently and gradually build up to a worthwhile level each day.

Start with five of the first three exercises and gradually build-up to fifteen or more a day.

Once you have developed a reasonable degree of fitness, you can then decide whether to continue the same routine (bearing in mind that routines do tend to get boring) or take up a new activity – maybe even go to the aerobics class!

SIT-UPS

Sit on the floor with feet apart, knees bent and arms at sides. Tighten stomach muscles and roll back slowly until you are lying on the floor with head slightly lifted. Roll back up again slowly, breathing out, until you reach sitting position, reaching forward with your arms.

WAIST STRETCHES

Stand with legs about a shoulder distance apart, knees slightly bent. Reach down to the right knee with your right hand making sure you keep upright and reach over your head with your left arm. Stretch as far as possible without straining. Repeat on the other side.

HEARTFELT BENEFIT

Exercise increases your fitness. It strengthens your heart muscles, improves your circulation and helps to reduce blood pressure and cholesterol levels

STAIR HOPS

Stand in front of the bottom stair. Step up, right leg leading, and stand on the stair for a moment before stepping down again. Build up to a good pace and start with at least ten. Aim to build up to 50 or more each day.

LEG STRETCHES

Lie on your side, supporting your head as shown. Bend the lower leg back from the knee and lift the top leg as far as it will comfortably stretch. Repeat on the other side.

"What else can I try?"

The simplest way to start boosting you daily activity is to increase the amount of time you spend walking. But don't stroll, walk briskly, striding out, arms swinging.

If you drive into town, park the car away from the centre and walk the rest of the way (you'll probably save money on parking as well!).

If you go by bus, get off at an earlier stop than usual.

If you have a dog (or if you know a man that does) then give it a treat. Go for a brisk walk and burn 80% of the energy that it would take to jog the same distance.

There are so many little ways in which you can effectively increase your daily activity.

Perhaps you could spread some of your shopping throughout the week so that you walk to the local store each day.

If you're faced with a choice, take the stairs to the upper floor instead of the lift. When you feel up to it, take two stairs at a time – it's really good exercise!

If you work in an office, try and escape at lunchtime and walk round the shops or a local park.

Remember, every bit of extra activity burns energy and boosts your BMR, so provided you're not eating more than you need, the extra energy will eventually come from your reserves of fat.

"So, is it really worth the effort?"

By exercising regularly you will become physically fitter and although you will use up more energy you will find that it is replaced more quickly so that you actually feel more energetic, less tired and generally brighter.

Indeed, exercise has a balancing effect on stress and anxiety. After all, it's difficult to stay anxious or angry while your mind and body are occupied with physical activity.

With vigorous exercise, powerful chemicals called endorphins are released by the brain. These act on the body in a similar way to morphine in producing a mental state of happiness and well-being.

People who do exercise regularly will certainly tell you that they feel better for it. Usually, they sleep more soundly, experience fewer aches and pains, feel generally calmer and have smaller appetites than inactive people.

So with the right attitude to diet and exercise you really can set yourself on a slimmer, healthier and happier course for life.

EXERCISE CAUTION

It's never too late to start exercising, but if you are seriously overweight, have suffered recent illness, have joint problems or have reached 40 or more, check with your doctor before you begin. Otherwise:

DO	start exercising slowly and build up gradually.
DON'T	push yourself to exhaustion. You should make yourself breathless but not speechless.
DO	warm up and gently stretch before exercising.
DON'T	stop suddenly, slow the pace to a comfortable level towards the end of your session.
DON'T	exercise after eating a meal, wait at least an hour before starting.
DON'T	ignore pain – your body is telling you to stop.

CHAPTER 12

Feeling great – looking good

*P*erhaps you should really wait for a week or two before reading this chapter, then you will be able to understand and appreciate the benefits of the Get Slim for Life programme.

If you *have* cut back dramatically on fats and sugar, increased your fibre intake and started regular exercise or activity you will certainly agree that you feel a different person.

Not only will you have shed a few pounds of fat but you will be fitter and more energetic. And if you hadn't noticed it yourself, your friends will probably begin to remark on the changes!

As we've stressed throughout the book, this diet is about a permanent change in lifestyle and not a get-slim-quick fad.

To summarise, these are the changes that you should now be making to your lifestyle:

Ten points for success

1. Avoid saturated fat as far as possible and keep intake of all fats to a minimum.

2. Avoid refined sugar whenever possible.

3. Keep up a healthy intake of dietary fibre.

4. Use fresh, unprocessed, ingredients as much as you can.
5. Try to keep to 3 meals a day, but if you need a snack, stick to the right kind of foods.
6. Eat moderate portions – try to eat slowly and chew thoroughly, so that you feel satisfied sooner and avoid over-eating. But don't starve yourself – it only means cravings later.
7. Maintain the recommended level of exercise and arrange your day to include plenty of activity – not just exercise – but interesting tasks that will stop you thinking about eating.
8. Drink plenty of water and fruit juice. Not only does it help to keep your appetite under control but it helps 'flush out' bodily wastes and toxins.
9. Enjoy your food. Make the effort to select fresh ingredients, to try new recipes, to taste exotic fruit and vegetables. Take time to enjoy your meals sitting at the table – don't rush around or watch TV – appreciate what you have prepared.
10. Reward your progress. Celebrate your better shape with some new clothes or an evening out. Take advantage of being slimmer and fitter – book an activity holiday or re-awaken your love life!

By following this advice you should certainly be losing weight after a week or two and it will be fat. You will have enjoyed good food without starving yourself and the old cravings for chips, cream cakes or chocolate will be gradually disappearing along with the excess fat.

Understand too, that this diet brings better health and greater fitness – in time. It takes several weeks to bring about a noticeable improvement in fitness but once you get going the results can be remarkable.

It may seem incredibly difficult at the moment to start putting some of these food and exercise ideas into action but don't be discouraged, start the changes gradually if you need to, but don't lose sight of the real aims.

Once you do get started, it's surprising how much easier it becomes day-by-day to adopt the healthier habits that promise a slimmer figure and much greater vitality. So what are you waiting for? Isn't it time you started the path to feeling and looking better – the path that you will enjoy for a lifetime!

Food Contents Tables

Use the following tables as a guide to the fibre, sugar and fat content of most types of food. Remember to keep saturated fats and sugar levels as low as possible. Figures are shown as grams/100 grams.

VEGETABLES (boiled unless otherwise indicated)	FIBRE	CARBOHYDRATES SUGAR	CARBOHYDRATES STARCH	FATS SAT FAT	FATS MONO FAT	FATS POLY FAT	TOTAL FAT
Globe Artichoke							
Jerusalem Artichoke				*Vegetables are virtually free*			
Asparagus	1.5	1.1		*of fat so only total levels are*			
Broad beans	4.2	0.6	6.5	*shown where present*			0.6
French beans	3.2	0.8	0.3				
Runner beans	3.4	1.3	1.4				0.2
Broccoli	4.1	1.5	0.1				
Brussels Sprouts	2.9	1.6	0.1				
White Cabbage (raw)	2.7	3.7	0.1				
White Cabbage	2.8	2.2	0.1				
Carrot (raw)	2.9	5.4					
Carrot	3.1	4.2	0.1				
Cauliflower (raw)	2.1	1.5					
Cauliflower	1.8	0.8					
Celery (raw)	1.8	1.2	0.1				
Celery	2.2	0.7					
Cucumber (raw)	0.4	1.8					0.1
Leeks	3.9	4.6					
Lettuce (raw)	1.5	1.2					
Marrow	0.6	1.3	0.1				
Mushroom	2.5						0.6
Onion (raw)	1.3	5.2					
Parsnip	2.5	2.7	10.8				
Peas (frozen)	12.0	1.0	3.3				0.4
Peas	5.2	1.8	5.9				0.4
Peppers (raw)	0.9	2.2					0.4
Potatoes (baked)	2.5	0.6	24.4				0.1
Potatoes	1.0	0.4	19.3				0.1

VEGETABLES (continued)	FIBRE	CARBOHYDRATES		FATS			TOTAL FAT
		SUGAR	STARCH	SAT FAT	MONO FAT	POLY FAT	
Spinach	6.3	1.2	0.2				0.5
Spring greens	3.8	0.9					
Swedes	2.8	3.7	0.1				
Sweetcorn	4.7	1.7	21.1				2.4
Tomatoes (raw)	1.5	2.8					
Tomatoes (tinned)	0.9	2.0					
Watercress (raw)	3.3	0.6	0.1				

FRUIT *Fruit is virtually free of fat except for the two items shown*

	FIBRE	SUGAR	STARCH	SAT FAT	MONO FAT	POLY FAT	TOTAL FAT
Apples (stewed)	2.1	7.9	0.3				
Apples	2.0	11.8	0.1				
Apricots (stewed)	1.7	5.6					
Apricots	2.1	6.7					
Apricots (dried)	24.0	43.3					
Apricots (dried, stewed)	8.9	16.1					
Avocado	2.0	1.8					22.2
Bananas	3.4	16.2	3.0				
Blackberries (stewed)	6.3	5.5					
Cherries	1.7	11.9					
Blackcurrants (stewed)	7.4	5.6					
Dates (dried)	8.7	63.9					
Figs	2.5	9.5					
Figs (dried)	18.5	52.9					
Gooseberries (stewed)	2.7	2.9					
Grapes, white	0.9	16.1					
Grapefruit	0.6	5.3					
Honeydew Melon	0.9	5.0					
Olives (bottled in brine)	4.4						11.0
Oranges	2.0	8.5					
Passion fruit	15.9	6.2					
Peaches	1.4	9.1					

	FIBRE	CARBOHYDRATES		FATS			TOTAL FAT
FRUIT *(continued)*		SUGAR	STARCH	SAT FAT	MONO FAT	POLY FAT	
Pears	2.3	10.6					
Pears (stewed)	2.5	7.9					
Pineapple	1.2	11.6					
Plums	2.1	9.6					
Plums (stewed)	2.2	5.2					
Prunes (stewed)	8.1	20.4					
Raisins	6.8	64.4					
Raspberries	7.4	5.6					
Rhubarb (stewed)	2.4	0.9					
Strawberries	2.2	6.2					
Sultanas	7.0	64.7					
Tangerines	1.9	8.0					
NUTS *(natural)*							
Almonds	14.3	4.3					53.5
Brazil Nuts	9.0	1.7	2.4				61.5
Chestnuts	6.8	7.0	29.6				2.7
Hazel Nuts	6.1	4.7	2.1				36.0
Coconut	13.6	3.7					36.0
Peanuts	8.1	3.1	5.5				49.0
Walnuts	5.2	3.2	1.8				51.5
JAMS & CONFECTIONERY *(You can see why they're best avoided!)*							
Golden Syrup		79.0					
Honey		76.4					
Jam (average)		69.0					
Boiled sweets		86.9					
Milk chocolate		56.5					30.3
Plain chocolate		59.5					29.2
Filled chocolates (average)		65.8					18.8
Toffees		70.1					17.2
CEREALS, CAKES & BISCUITS				*All cereal is mainly mono/polyunsaturated fats, as per example below*			
Flour (wholemeal)	9.6	2.3	63.5				2.0
Flour (plain, white)	3.4	1.7	78.4				1.2
Oatmeal	7.0		72.8	1.61	3.35	3.73	8.7

CEREALS, CAKES & BISCUITS (continued)	FIBRE	CARBOHYDRATES		FATS			TOTAL FAT
		SUGAR	STARCH	SAT FAT	MONO FAT	POLY FAT	
Rice (white, cooked)	0.8		29.6				0.3
Rice (wholemeal, cooked)	1.5		32.1				1.1
Pasta (white, cooked)			25.2				0.3
Pasta (wholemeal, cooked)	3.4		25.0				0.9
Bread (white)	2.7	1.8	47.9				1.7
Bread (brown)	5.1	1.8	42.9				2.2
Bread (wholemeal)	8.5	2.1	39.7				2.7
BREAKFAST CEREALS							
All-Bran	26.7	15.4	27.6				5.7
Cornflakes	11.0	7.4	77.7				1.6
Muesli (average)	7.4	26.2	40.0				7.5
Puffed wheat	15.4	1.5	67.0				1.3
Rice krispies	4.5	9.0	79.1				2.0
Shredded Wheat	12.3	0.4	67.5				3.0
Sugar Puffs	6.1	56.5	28.0				0.8
Weetabix	12.7	6.1	66.5				3.4
BISCUITS							
Water biscuits	3.2	2.3	73.5				12.5
Cream crackers	3.0		68.3				16.3
Crispbread (average)	11.7	3.2	67.4	*Cakes and biscuits are mainly saturated and mono unsaturated fats as per the examples below*			2.1
Digestive (plain)	5.5	16.4	49.6				20.5
Digestive (chocolate)	3.5	28.5	38.0				24.1
Ginger Nuts	2.0	35.8	43.3	7.52	6.08	1.46	15.2
Shortbread	2.1	17.2	48.3				26.0
CAKES							
Victoria jam sponge	1.2	47.7	16.5	10.6	10.91	4.5	26.5
Chocolate Eclairs		26.3	11.9				24.0
Fruit cake (plain)	2.8	43.1	14.8	6.07	5.44	1.18	12.9
Gingerbread	1.3	31.8	30.9				12.6
Doughnuts		15.0	33.8				15.8

Food Contents Tables

CAKES (continued)	FIBRE	CARBOHYDRATES		FATS			TOTAL FAT
		SUGAR	STARCH	SAT FAT	MONO FAT	POLY FAT	
Mince pies	2.9	30.0	31.7				20.7
Scones	2.1	6.1	49.8				14.0

DAIRY PRODUCTS

Milk (whole)		4.8		2.4	1.2	0.1	3.8
Milk (semi-skimmed)		5.0		1.0	0.5		1.5
Milk (skimmed)		4.8		0.1			0.1
Butter				54.0	19.8	2.6	82
Cheese (cheddar)		0.1		21.7	9.4	1.4	33.5
Cheese (Brie)				16.8	7.8	2.6	23.2
Cream cheese				29.7	13.7	1.4	47.4
Cheese (Feta)		1.5		13.7	4.1	0.6	18.5
Cottage Cheese		2.1		2.4	1.1	0.1	4.0
Clotted cream		2.3		39.7	18.4	1.8	59.9
Double cream		2.7		30.0	13.9	1.4	48.2
Single cream		4.1		11.9	5.5	0.5	21.1
Yoghurt		6.2		2.5	0.9	0.1	1.0
Eggs (boiled)				3.1	4.6	1.2	10.9
Eggs (fried – *approx fat content depending on type of fat used*)							19.5

PULSES (*cooked values*)

Butter beans	5.1	1.5	15.6				0.3
Haricot beans	7.4	0.8	15.8				0.5
Lentils	3.7	0.8	16.2				0.5
Split peas	5.1	0.9	21.0				0.3

OILS

Corn oil				12.7	24.2	58.7	
Olive oil				13.5	73.7	8.4	
Safflower				9.1	12.1	74.5	
Sesame				14.2	39.7	41.7	
Sunflower				10.3	19.5	65.7	

FISH (*steamed unless otherwise indicated*)

Cod					0.9
Haddock				*Fish and shellfish are generally low in fat which is mainly mono or polyunsaturated*	0.8
Halibut					4.0
Lemon Sole					0.9

FISH *(continued)*	FIBRE	CARBOHYDRATES		FATS			TOTAL FAT
^	^	SUGAR	STARCH	SAT FAT	MONO FAT	POLY FAT	^
Plaice							1.9
Whiting							0.9
Herring (grilled)							13.0
Mackerel (grilled)							11.3
Salmon							13.0
Salmon (smoked)							4.5
Trout							4.5

SHELLFISH *(boiled, unless specified)*

Crab							5.2
Lobster							3.4
Prawns							1.8
Shrimps							2.4
Cockles							0.3
Mussels							2.0
Oysters (raw)							0.9
Scallops (steamed)							1.4

MEAT *You can see the value in choosing leaner cuts and avoiding saturated fat.*

Beef							
Average rump steak, grilled				5.44	5.96	0.69	12.1
Lean rump steak, grilled				2.7	2.96	0.04	6.0
Average mince, stewed				6.9	7.5	0.86	15.2
Lean mince, stewed				2.7	2.96	0.04	6.0
Average sirloin, roast				9.5	10.4	1.2	21.1
Lean sirloin, roast				4.1	4.48	0.51	9.1
Lamb							
Average chops, grilled				15.2	12	1.5	29.0
Lean chops, grilled				6.5	5.04	0.61	12.3
Average leg, roast				9.4	7.4	0.9	17.9
Lean leg, roast				4.3	3.3	0.4	8.1
Average shoulder, roast				13.75	10.8	1.3	26.3

		CARBOHYDRATES		FATS			
MEAT *(continued)*	FIBRE	SUGAR	STARCH	SAT FAT	MONO FAT	POLY FAT	
Lean shoulder, roast				5.9	4.6	0.6	11.2
Average breast, roast				18.1	14.2	1.75	34.6
Lean breast, roast				8.7	6.8	0.8	16.6
Pork							
Average chops, grilled				10.4	11.6	2.1	24.2
Lean chops, grilled				4.6	5.1	0.9	10.7
Average leg, roast				8.5	9.5	1.8	19.8
Lean leg, roast				2.96	3.31	0.6	6.9
Ham				2.2	2.44	0.46	5.1
Back Bacon, lean rashers fried				9.88	10.7	1.74	22.3
Back Bacon, lean + fat rashers fried				17.58	19.48	3.16	40.6
Back Bacon, lean rashers grilled				8.31	9.07	1.51	18.9
Back Bacon, lean + fat rashers grilled				14.87	16.22	0.57	33.8
Veal							
Fillet, roast				5.17	5.75	0.57	11.5
POULTRY & GAME							
Chicken							
Roast, with skin				4.9	6.72	2.1	14.0
Roast, meat only				1.9	2.6	0.8	5.4
Duck							
Roast, with skin				8.41	16.53	1.69	29.0
Roast, meat only				2.81	5.53	1.26	9.7
Grouse							
Roast, meat only				1.32	0.69	3.28	5.3
Partridge							
Roast, meat only				2.0	3.5	1.8	7.2
Pheasant							
Roast, meat only				3.25	4.83	1.2	9.3
Turkey							
Roast, with skin				2.4	1.8	2.0	6.5

POULTRY & GAME (continued)	FIBRE	CARBOHYDRATES		FATS			TOTAL FAT
		SUGAR	STARCH	SAT FAT	MONO FAT	POLY FAT	
Turkey							
Roast, meat only				1.0	1.8	0.8	2.7
Rabbit							
Stewed				2.9	2.0	2.7	7.7
Venison							
Roast				*	*	*	6.4
MEAT PRODUCTS							
Corned Beef			0.0				12.1
Luncheon Meat			5.5				26.9
Liver Sausage			4.3				26.9
Frankfurters			3.0				25.0
Salami			1.9				45.2
Pork Sausages (grilled)			11.5				24.6
Beef sausages			15.2				18.0
Beefburgers, fried			7.0				17.3
Cornish pastie			31.1				20.4
Sausage roll			33.1				36.2
Pork Pie			24.9				27.0

* *figures not available*

Further reading

Cookery and food preparation

Therer are many excellent books on cookery methods, from Mrs Beeton onwards, but one worth mentioning is the Readers Digest Complete Guide to Cookery.

Recipes

Over the years a number of slimmer's cookbooks have been published, many with low-fat recipes and some with low sugar. Often, artificial sweetener is substituted for sugar in such recipes but even this should really be avoided since it doesn't re-educate your taste buds to avoid sweet foods.

Two recipe books that you might like to try are Good Housekeeping's Low Calorie Cookbook (Ebury Press) and the Hamlyn All Colour Slimming Cookbook.